The Search for

THE UNDERGROUND

RAILROAD

IN SOUTH-CENTRAL

–OHIO–

The Search for

THE UNDERGROUND

RAILROAD

IN SOUTH-CENTRAL

-OHIO-

TOM CALARCO

THE
History
PRESS

Published by The History Press
Charleston, SC
www.historypress.com

First published 2018

Manufactured in the United States

ISBN 9781467140102

Library of Congress Control Number: 2018947022

CONTENTS

PREFACE

It is surprising that a book focusing on the Underground Railroad (UGRR) in south-central Ohio has not been written. The UGRR is a weighty subject that covers a period of sixty years involving thousands of persons and events that deserve further study, and even this relatively small geographic area supplies enough material for many books. This slim volume makes no pretense at full coverage of such a huge topic covering many years. It simply will lift the essence of its memories and provide highlights. Its significance is that it will show through them the truth of the UGRR. I hope that it will encourage others to pick up where it has left off, to enlighten us with the huge chunk of history yet to be told. Posterity compels the deeds of these good country people to live on. It should entice scholars, genealogists, history buffs, teachers and students.

The author often quotes contemporary accounts or those of witnesses to the history. For the sake of euphony and clarity, he has taken the liberty of correcting punctuation and spelling and sometimes omitting needless words and phrases.

INTRODUCTION

T here are many forsaken tracks of history—some that will never be recovered and others whose trail can be at least partially restored. One of them is the neglected story of the UGRR so active in the communities stretching north of the Ohio River to northwest and northeast of Columbus. Recent books like Ann Hagedorn's *Beyond the River*, Keith Griffler's *Frontline of Freedom*, Nikki Taylor's *Frontiers of Freedom* and Gary Knepp's *Freedom's Struggle* have provided good coverage of activities along the river towns from Cincinnati to Ripley. But no major work, aside from the 1951 *Ohio's Mysteries of the Underground Railroad* by Wilbur Siebert, has been written of the netherworld between the Ohio River and Lake Erie, the final destination before reaching the Promised Land of Canada.

Siebert has lost some credibility over the years due to revisionist theories that began with Larry Gara's *Liberty Line*, published in 1961. The most substantial statewide coverage since then is the Ohio Underground Railroad Association's survey of sites coordinated by Cathy Nelson and published in 2004. Other contributions advancing our knowledge of the state's UGRR have been made by Henry Burke of southeastern Ohio; Cheryl Janifer LaRoche and her work on selected African American communities in the Midwest; Beverly J. Gray, whose blogs feature African American contributions; Karen S. Campbell's research detailing Quaker participation; Wayne L. Snider's collection of African American oral tradition in southeastern Ohio; Paul Larue's Washington Court House High School research of Fayette County; the Mary S. Cook Library review of Warren County; and the Greenfield

Historical Society's detailed analysis of Highland County, as well as efforts by local historians in Cincinnati, Sandusky, Hudson and Mount Pleasant, Ohio, among others.[1] This book shall integrate these works and provide a more unified picture of the UGRR in the south-central region of Ohio.

As the Ohio River formed the borderline between slavery and freedom, fugitives from slavery sought to cross it. Naturally, once across, they were going to need help to get to Canada or to live in the North as free persons. The river towns played an important role as destinations and centers where help could be found. But who helped those thousands once they left to journey farther north? Their story will be told here, sometimes in their own words, and rely on antebellum documents and primary sources.

Chapter 1

THE SO-CALLED ROMANTIC ADVENTURE STORY OF ADDISON WHITE AND UDNEY HYDE

H istory cannot be rewritten with a view to popular opinion or judged by today's standards. This distorts the true understanding of the people and the events. To experience it, we need to walk in the shoes of those of the past—to hear their words, to feel their emotions.

On May 19, 1857, Udney Hyde, a UGRR veteran in Mechanicsburg, Ohio, a village in Champaign County situated between Columbus and Dayton, was recuperating from a broken ankle. He also was harboring a fugitive slave from Kentucky, thirty-five-year-old Addison White, a powerfully built man known for his prodigious strength. It was daybreak, and the roosters were crowing and the sun peeking over the horizon. It was cold, and there was a drizzle of rain. A posse of six slave catchers led by U.S. Deputies Ben P. Churchill and John C. Elliott of Cincinnati and Champaign County sheriff John Puffinbarger approached the Hyde log cabin in two carriages. They were about a mile or so outside the town.[2]

White's whereabouts had been pinpointed thanks to the interception of letters between White and his family in Kentucky by Springfield, Ohio postmaster W.G. Boggs. For weeks, Puffinbarger had been scoping out the area and had a sent a spy to apply for temporary work with Hyde. He confirmed the presence of White.[3]

There are numerous stories about what happened. One was provided by Hyde's daughter, Amanda, who was fourteen at the time and was an eyewitness. What follows is taken from her account and others, notably the newspaper transcripts of the trials that followed and which were reported

Udney Hyde. *Courtesy Ohio History Center.*

in great detail in the newspapers of that time. A great deal of conflicting testimony was given and this writer has made some reasonable conclusions as to the turn of events, but generally they present a fair likelihood of what happened. Perhaps as many as one hundred reports were published in various newspapers of the time, including the *New York Tribune.*[4]

White was already up and stoking the fireplace that morning, next to the bed of Hyde, who was still asleep. The sound of hoofbeats preceded the posse, and he was the first to hear the commotion outside. He peered out and saw the men and carriages. In his bedroom, the sleep of Hyde was stirred. White jumped into the loft, where he slept, carrying a revolver.

The marshals knocked, but there was no answer. They shouted and banged, but still no answer. They started kicking at the door and kept at it until the door crashed open. Hyde now was wide awake. A few others were trying to get in through the back door; Hyde pushed his bed against it. He demanded that they leave, that they had no right to break into his home. They asked Hyde about White, but he didn't answer. Then they heard movement above. Elliott called up to Add. Hyde warned him that Add was fully prepared to defend himself. The marshals looked at one another with concern; they knew of Add's reputation as a kind of modern-day Samson. Elliott fired his double-barreled shotgun up through the ceiling. The blast dissipated into silence. It seemed to grow thicker. Elliott hesitated and then slowly proceeded up the ladder to the loft, holding his gun up around his head. He peeked over the edge of the ceiling and met with a shot from Add's revolver that careened off Elliott's shotgun and grazed his cheek and ear. He fell back and cried out, "I'm a dead man."[5]

All the marshals fled, and Elliott followed them. Hyde's youngest son, who also lived in the cabin, had been seized when he tried to run for help, so he directed Amanda to go to her older brother Russell's home a short distance and rally the locals. When she stepped outside, the marshals asked why her father was laid up. On impulse, she told them he had smallpox.[6]

Addison White.
Courtesy Ohio History Center.

Quickly, she raced to her brother's nearby homestead, ignoring the angry shouts of the marshals. Like Paul Revere, Russell Hyde sped off on horseback and awakened the still sleeping village of Mechanicsburg. The marshals parleyed about their next move. Elliott said that if anyone else wanted to go and confront White, they were welcome, but there were no takers. Before long, about ten or so villagers had arrived armed with clubs and pitchforks, followed by Russell with a half dozen more, as well as neighbor Nelson Downey. The villagers had the advantage of numbers but not weapons, the marshals each having at least two revolvers. It was probably similar to the scene in Christiana, Pennsylvania, in 1851 when the slaveholders supported by U.S. marshals attempted the rendition of the slave William Parker, although the crowd there was probably larger and more intimidating and Parker's homestead was fortified with a cache of weapons. The villagers gave them five minutes to leave. The marshals decided to comply.[7]

Eight days passed before the U.S. marshals led by Churchill and Elliott returned to Mechanicsburg. It was a Wednesday, and both Udney Hyde and Addison White had gone into hiding. Some said that Add had gone on the UGRR to Canada, while Hyde was staying close by, visiting friends for meals and other necessities but spending most of his time in a nearby swamp. The marshals had arrived by train in Urbana on Monday evening and had warrants for the arrest of Hyde and others for violations of the fugitive slave law (see the appendix for more information). The posse included ten officers in all, five marshals and five assistants. In a buggy and three carriages, they went directly to Hyde's cabin, where they found his eldest son, Russell, who had begun staying there since his father went into hiding, and promptly arrested him without resistance. Then they went and arrested Charles Taylor, whom they learned had written those letters to White's wife in Kentucky.

From the Citizen & Gazette, May 22, 1857.

After giving Taylor time to gather himself, they headed through Mechanicsburg, where a large crowd blocked the roadway. Among them were Edward Taylor, Charles's brother, and Hiram Guthridge. Charles called out to them. Edward and Hiram approached the lead buggy in which sat Elliott and Churchill. They began demanding the release of Charles. Some of the other marshals left their carriages and surrounded them. Churchill shouted to arrest them. The crowd jeered, and Ed Pangborn, who was among them, shouted, "Stop them!" Churchill cautioned the crowd and got out of the buggy. He held up his hands and told the people not to worry, that they were taking the men to Urbana, where they would get a fair hearing. The crowd murmured but parted, and the posse proceeded out of town. Quickly, Oliver Caldwell and some others assembled, including Russell Hyde's father-in-law, Clinton Buffington; all agreed they needed to follow the marshals. Most went to retrieve their horses. Caldwell had a coach and Buffington a buggy. They followed, with Caldwell taking the lead and Buffington the rear.

As the posse proceeded, the men came upon Mechanicsburg attorney David Rutan on horseback, heading toward town. Rutan looked at them with concern and up the road met the villagers who were following. He decided to join them and hitched up his horse to Caldwell's carriage. The villagers had tried to maintain a good distance, but when the posse turned south, the bend in the road brought them into view and Churchill stopped it. Churchill got out of his buggy, and some of the other marshals followed. They watched as the caravan of townspeople approached. Caldwell continued toward them, concerned that the posse had turned in the opposite direction of Urbana. He finally stopped when they were within hearing distance.

"What in the devil are you following us for?" Churchill asked.

"To see fair play," Rutan said.

The marshals looked at one another and shook their heads. One of them carrying a billy club had slipped by unnoticed and skulked up behind Caldwell. "Damn you!" said the marshal, who knocked Caldwell in the back. "Turn your horse and clear yourself, or take a damned flogging!"

Caldwell started to pull out his pistol but was restrained by Rutan.

Churchill pulled out his revolver and pointed it at the villagers as he spoke. "If you want to stay alive, I'd advise you to turn around now."[8]

They complied, and Caldwell took off for Urbana, about five miles to the north, to get a writ of habeas corpus.[9]

After some hours, the slave catchers stopped for dinner at a local inn in Vienna, about ten miles south of where they had confronted the villagers. While they placed the prisoners in an outhouse, they celebrated with rounds of hard liquor.[10] It was just as they were about to leave that Sheriff John Clark of Champaign County, who had in his possession a writ signed by Judge Samuel Baldwin, entered the inn, along with some others, including Hyde's neighbor, Nelson Downey. Clark discussed the situation with Churchill and told him that he had the writ, but because they were in Clark County, he didn't believe he had the power to enforce it. He informed Churchill that other sheriffs had received the writ and could enforce it if they were passing through their county. Churchill said he didn't care about writs, that they were acting under a higher authority. Deputy Traler scoffed, saying the writs were "worth no more than pieces of brown paper."

During the parley between the sheriff and marshal, Elliott confronted Downey, whom he recognized from the confrontation at Hyde's cabin. "You God Damn, scoundrel," he said. "You better watch yourself or I'm gonna cut your guts out!" Downing started to say something but was cut off by Elliott: "Don't open your mouth, or I'll knock your head off."

The slave catchers quickly left, laughing and uttering a stream of profanities.[11] They weren't on the road long before they saw a buggy racing toward them from the opposite direction. It was Sheriff John E. Layton of Clark County and his deputy William H. Compton. "They must be damn fools to attempt to rescue the prisoners with two men," Churchill said.

"Stop, stop, stop," Layton called. The marshals ignored them as the sheriff rode up alongside; Compton jumped out and raced over to the marshal's buggy, grabbing at his horse's reins. Elliott, who was driving, followed through with his whip across the head of the Compton, while Layton drove his buggy up to the carriage behind them and also tried to stop the marshal's carriage, with Elliott whipping Compton.

"Shoot the damn son of a bitch!" cried one of the marshals. Church and Elliott fired at Compton but missed. They all pulled to a halt, and Churchill and Layton got out of their buggies. The sheriff offered to show his writ.

"Go to Hell," Churchill said. "No Sheriff has the right to serve us a writ of habeas corpus." The sheriff went to take the writ out of his pocket, and some of the marshals thought he was reaching for his gun.

"Don't let the son of a bitch draw his pistol," they cried. "Kill him, shoot him."

Churchill attacked Layton and beat him with his billy club and the handle of his revolver. A few other marshals finished it off, severely kicking Layton in the chest as he lay on the ground. Then the marshals hurried off as some villagers, who had continued following, raced to the scene. Layton was still on the ground, bleeding profusely from his head and holding his chest.[12]

Now the chase had begun. But the good country people of Ohio were up to the task. A posse of sixty men, all armed and led by Sheriff Daniel Lewis of Greene County, caught up with them in Lumberton, just over the Greene County border in Clinton County. The marshals realized that they didn't have a chance against such numbers, especially with a large posse of citizens coming from another direction. Churchill and Elliott remained to face the music, while some of the others scattered. Eventually, all but one were caught. They were brought to Springfield, where they were incarcerated overnight. The following day, they were released on bail.[13]

In the next weeks, the original four Mechanicsburg men were charged with violations of the fugitive slave laws and the state law enforcement officials for obstructing justice. The judge presiding over the case against the marshals stood firmly on the side of the federal government, arguing that the state had no legal authority to issue a writ of habeas corpus for a lawful arrest—in this case an arrest by the federal government.[14] It was a battle of states' rights versus the federal government, a conflict that had been taking place throughout the North since the passage of the stronger FSL of 1850 and would continue until the Civil War. The comments of one of the prosecutors during the trial of the marshals provided an accurate forecast of the coming Civil War. The surprise is that they came from a northerner, an Ohio resident. It was a reflection of the long battle the abolitionists had been facing for nearly three decades and would continue to face until the war:

> [I] *have no apprehensions of civil war; but should it come, [I] have no doubt of the side upon which the greater position of the people should be found. The laws of the country should be supported at all hazards; all good citizens should shoulder a musket for the purpose; for once admit the law that Sheriff of Clark county, his underling, and the people of adjacent counties, being executed, and this country and government would be forever at an end.*[15]

As for Hyde and White, the conclusion of their tale will come later.

Chapter 2

THE TRUTH ABOUT THE UNDERGROUND RAILROAD

To the average American, the UGRR continues to be the story of a network of good Samaritans helping desperate humanity along various routes to freedom. This portrayal was developed mainly from the research of Wilbur Siebert, an Ohio State history professor, whose seminal work on the topic, *The Underground Railroad: From Freedom to Slavery*, was published in 1898.

For many years, information about the UGRR originated mostly from this book, based mainly on memories that Siebert had collected through his UGRR survey. His collection was part of a body of UGRR remembrances published mainly in the nineteenth century. Most notable were William Still's *The Underground Railroad: A Record*; Levi Coffin's *Reminiscences*; and Robert Smedley's *History of the Underground Railroad in Chester County, Pennsylvania*. All presented a story of a network of individuals, sometimes organized, who through various means aided tens of thousands obtain their freedom, with most ending up in Canada.

The roots of the UGRR harken back to the days of the American Revolution. Two letters written by George Washington in 1786 refer to the Society for the Relief of Free Negroes Unlawfully Held in Bondage, which was located in Philadelphia.[16] He speaks of a runaway who escaped to Philadelphia, where "a society of Quakers in the city…have attempted to liberate" him.[17]

As the name suggests, the focus of the society was to help free men who had been kidnapped into slavery, something that was not uncommon and was so well depicted in the classic tale of Solomon Northup. A picture of this first UGRR society and how it operated can be found in the memoirs of one of its members, Isaac T. Hopper, which were collected and turned into a book by abolitionist author Lydia Maria Child.[18] His tactics, which often shrewdly made use of the court system, were later emulated by others in their efforts to help slaves gain their freedom.

However, the UGRR of legend was still years in the making during the time of Washington. Two unrelated events in 1793 led to its eventual organization: Eli Whitney's cotton gin, which dramatically increased the production of cotton and the need for slave labor, and the fugitive slave laws (FSL) of 1793, which imposed a fine of $500 for each runaway slave aided by those convicted.[19]

But this first national fugitive slave law did not work well for slave owners. The American judiciary was in its infancy, and the travel and time needed to apprehend slaves was expensive. The law also was cumbersome and inconvenient—it was hard to locate judges to administer it. So, slaveholders became dependent on slave catchers. These mercenaries had no ethics, and their nefarious work expanded into kidnapping free people of color. By 1796, the annual number of such kidnappings was reported to be in the hundreds.[20] The banning of international slave trade in 1808, which had provided a continual source of slaves, didn't help matters. These slave catchers operated mainly along the borders between the North and the South. One kidnapping ring, the Patty Cannon Gang, included more than thirty members working between Virginia and Philadelphia.[21] The kidnappings also were common along the Ohio River Valley, especially in southern Illinois, which was extremely proslavery.[22] Although laws were passed in both the North and South to prohibit the kidnappings, they continued until the end of slavery.

Slaves were constantly trying to escape, and no wonder. It seems ridiculous in retrospect that some historians have tried to persuade us that the slaves were mostly content. Evidence showing their discontent is the estimated 100,000 ads for runaways that still exist in surviving antebellum newspapers.[23]

The harshness of slavery in the South was revealed by a former slave who became a prosperous Rochester grocer. Austin Steward had fled from slavery after his family's master had moved his entire plantation from Virginia to upstate New York. In 1857, he wrote his autobiography and described the conditions working in the fields:

> *Capt. H. employed an overseer* [who] *always went around with a whip, about nine feet long...the butt-end of which was loaded with lead...*

running to a point at the opposite extremity....With it, the skin of an ox or a horse could be cut through....Our overseer, thus armed with his cowhide, and with a large bulldog behind him, followed the slaves all day; if one of them fell in the rear from any cause, this cruel weapon was plied with terrible force.

That was an ordinary day in the fields. Real punishment was much worse. The slaves were made to lay bare back, their hands tied behind them. The end of the rope was tossed over a beam, and then they were drawn up until they stood on the tips of their toes. Sometimes a rail was placed between their legs, which were then tied tightly together. Thirty-nine lashes was the minimum. Blood would begin flow, but the overseer wouldn't stop until he reached the number. Some died from the floggings, and some slaves were executed in this manner, being flogged until they bled to death.[24]

Despite the pain, suffering, squalid living conditions, meager diet and demeaning social status that most slaves faced, the most compelling reason for flight was separation of family. It was why many slaves who enjoyed privileges given to few others sometimes took flight, like the famed Henry "Box" Brown.

The Hermitage Plantation, Louisa County, Virginia, birthplace of Henry "Box" Brown. *Courtesy of Tom Calarco.*

HENRY "BOX" BROWN

Brown was born at the Hermitage, a tobacco plantation of "benevolent" slave owner John Barret, in Louisa County, Virginia, about forty-five miles northwest of Richmond. He had it easy for a slave. He worked primarily in the main house, waiting on his master's family, and was a favorite of his master. He was always nicely dressed and fed well, and his family members were not separated during his youth. His master always promised that he would free him when he grew up. But his master died before that time, and he became the slave of one of his master's sons.

The son lived in Richmond and operated the family tobacco factory. Henry was moved there and put to work in the factory. He was given lodgings in a rooming house. After some time, Henry was given the freedom to live in his own apartment. He also was given a salary, eventually married, had three children and became of member of the African Baptist Church choir. It was an almost idyllic situation for a slave.

There was just one problem. His wife and children were owned by a different master, who could sell them and send them away forever if he desired. The Browns lived in constant fear of this, and sure enough, one day at work, Henry learned the horrifying news: his wife and children were to be sold away. A friend learned that they were going to be sent to North Carolina in a coffle gang.

The next day, Henry stationed himself along the street where they were to pass:

> Soon [I] had the melancholy satisfaction of witnessing the approach of a gang of slaves, amounting to three hundred and fifty in number....I stood in the midst of many who, like myself, were mourning the loss of friends and relations.... [They] were marched with ropes about their necks, and staples on their arms, and...this train of beings was accompanied by a number of wagons loaded with little children of many different families, which as they appeared rent the air with their shrieks and cries and vain endeavors to resist the separation...but what should I now see in the very foremost wagon but a little child looking towards me and pitifully calling, father! father!...My eldest child....My wife...jumped aside; I seized hold of her hand while my mind felt unutterable things, and my tongue was only able to say, we shall meet in heaven! I went with her for about four miles hand in hand, but both our hearts were so overpowered with feeling that we could say nothing.[25]

On that day, he made his resolution to escape from slavery. Little did he realize that he would never see his family again. On March 23, 1849, he undertook his scheme to be shipped to freedom in a box. He had two accomplices who shipped him: James Caesar Anthony Smith, a free black member of Henry's church, and Samuel Anderson Smith, a four-foot-nine dandy and maverick gambler. A shoe dealer by trade, Samuel had a history of helping slaves escape.

For twenty-seven hours, Brown remained in the box during a journey that took him 250 miles to the vigilance committee office in Philadelphia. Despite sometimes being placed upside down and with only a small air hole that had been cut into the box through which to breathe, he survived to become one of the most celebrated of all fugitives from slavery.

The nostalgic picture of the contented slave who roamed the plantations singing "Dixie" was one of the greatest myths ever perpetrated, as in the legendary *Gone with the Wind*. Among the earliest Underground Railroad stops was in Wrightsville, Pennsylvania, along the Susquehanna River near the Maryland border, where the mother-in-law of UGRR conductor William Whipper was the first reported escaped slave in 1804.[26] Along the Ohio River Valley, fugitives began coming after the battles of the War of 1812 brought to slaves the awareness of freedom north of the Mason-Dixon line when they accompanied masters who were fighting in the war.[27] Because of their insularity and illiteracy, slaves had little knowledge of what existed beyond the plantation and were told absurd stories—like, for instance, that abolitionists were cannibals.[28]

Before 1831, when William Lloyd Garrison had launched the publication of *The Liberator* calling for immediate emancipation, more than 85 percent of the more than one hundred abolitionist societies that existed were in the South.[29] Among them was the New Garden Quaker meeting of Levi Coffin's youth in Guilford County, North Carolina, where fugitives were being assisted before 1820.[30] But the slave revolts gradually stymied this movement in the South. The most important and the coup de grâce was the Nat Turner Rebellion in Virginia, which occurred less than a year after the launching of *The Liberator*.

Although born a slave, Turner was taught as a child that he was destined to be a prophet and would lead the slaves to freedom like Moses did for the Jews. He was a precocious boy who taught himself to read and grew into a man with an uncommon degree of self-importance and a belief in his destiny. Fittingly, he became a preacher.

At the age of twenty-five, he sensed that the time was coming for it to be fulfilled, and he withdrew and immersed himself in prayer and fasting. On the

Depiction of the Nat Turner Massacre. *Library of Congress.*

night of August 22, 1831, he and six other slaves began their rampage. Armed with guns, swords and axes, they began to massacre every white person, regardless of sex or age, in their path. They started with Turner's master and continued on from one plantation to the next, butchering white people in their beds. As they proceeded, they were joined by many of the slaves freed during the rampage, and his band at one point totaled fifty or more.

Word of their massacre quickly spread, and before long, they were confronted by the state militia, whose superior numbers overwhelmed them. In all, they had murdered fifty people. But Turner escaped. He was able to stay hidden for more than two months before he was finally discovered. On November 11, 1831, he was hanged in Jerusalem, Virginia, after which his body was skinned.

The massacre terrified the South. The climate of fear that it created is reflected in this excerpt from James McDowell's address in 1832 at the Virginia House of Delegates:

> *We are in peril of our lives*—[the Turner affair has]…*banished every sense of security from every man's dwelling….Was it the fear of Nat. Turner…which produced such effects?…..No, sir, it was the suspicion eternally attached to the slave himself; the suspicion that a Nat Turner might be in every family—that the same bloody deed might be acted over at any time, and in any place—that the materials for it were spread through the land, and were always ready for a like explosion.*[31]

Consequently, more repressive laws regarding slaves were passed throughout the South. Preachers of color, like Turner, were no longer allowed to conduct religious services without the presence of a white person. In some cases, people of color were not even permitted to have their own churches and were required to go to white churches, where they were placed in segregated pews. Laws to restrict the meeting of groups of people of color both slave and free were also put in effect, as well as greater restrictions on their freedom of movement. Other laws prevented the sale of guns or liquor to people of color. But of even greater significance in relation to the UGRR was that antislavery societies in the South ceased to exist. Nightly slave patrols increased to prevent the flight of slaves, and gradually, the South turned into an increasingly repressive police state.[32]

The Turner Rebellion, which occurred only nine months after Garrison launched *The Liberator*, made things difficult for him, and he depended greatly on the subscriptions of free people of color at that time.[33] But with the formation of the American Anti-Slavery Society in 1833, led by Garrison, auxiliary branches began to form and multiplied through the outreach efforts of Theodore Weld and his band of seventy lecturers from 1835 to 1837, all of whom spread the abolitionist message throughout the North and established networks from which the UGRR as we have come to know it was established.[34]

By 1850, its successes had led to the passage of an even more vigorous Fugitive Slave Act that gave the federal government more power to enforce the law against those in the UGRR. Not only did it double the fine charged for helping fugitives, but it also made the law less difficult to enforce by appointing special commissioners to adjudge the cases, adding a monetary incentive if a guilty verdict was found.[35] Most noxious of all to northerners was a requirement to aid law enforcement officials in the apprehension of a fugitive from slavery under the same penalty as those who willfully harbored or helped them escape. As many abolitionists commented at the time, it turned everyone into a slave catcher.

The UGRR was never monolithic but rather continually changing, adapting to the situation and technological advances of its time. For instance, in addition to using false-bottom and covered wagons, boats, skiffs and steamers, it also made use of the "upperground" railroad and the newly invented telegraph, which made its debut in 1844. This was mainly used by UGRR centers in the cities, which had better access to it. UGRR conductors William Still in Philadelphia and Sidney Howard Gay in New York City were among those who used it.

On August 17, 1855, Gay wrote in a letter to Still, "In special cases you might advise me by Telegraph." In Still's account book, he noted that he dispatched telegraphs to Gay on November 1 and 9, 1855, and March 31 and June 4, 1856.[36]

The UGRR also was empowered by the antislavery newspapers that spread the news of its successes. They, of course, had firsthand accounts because most of them were not only stops on the UGRR but also central dissemination points. Among the notable newspapers whose offices functioned as centers of the UGRR were *The Liberator* in Boston, the *National Anti-Slavery Standard* and *True Wesleyan* in New York, the *Pennsylvania Freeman* in Philadelphia, the *North Star* (later *Frederick Douglass's Paper*) in Rochester, the *Tocsin of Liberty/Albany Patriot* in Albany, the *Western Citizen* in Chicago and the *Anti-Slavery Bugle* in Salem, Ohio.[37] Invariably, if one digs deeper, he or she will find that wherever there was an antislavery publication, there was the UGRR. So deeply involved were these activist journalists that some revisionist historians have suggested that the UGRR was as much about propaganda as actual work to aid fugitives from slavery (see *Liberty Line* by Larry Gara).

But best of all, its army of Samaritans were all-volunteer. It had many thoroughfares and routes that were ever changing because of people moving or dying, routes being co-opted or just the evolution of the transportation systems. Sometimes a sympathetic neighbor who was not part of the network would be called on and willing to give a hand. Naturally, the methods and itineraries had much to do with geography. On the East Coast—especially in Virginia and the ports of Richmond, Portsmouth and Norfolk, which had a huge shipping trade with New York and Boston—oceangoing vessels were used.[38] This was a natural choice because most seamen of the day on American ships were men of color and would hide fugitives without knowledge of their captains.

Inland waterways also served as important thoroughfares, especially during the UGRR's early years. The Ohio, Susquehanna, Hudson and Connecticut Rivers were used along with the widespread auxiliary canal systems that began to develop during the 1820s. In the South, the prevalence of using slaves as boatmen played an important role in the flight of numerous fugitive slaves.[39] By the late 1830s, the steamers and schooners plying the waters of Lake Erie and Lake Ontario were carrying hundreds to freedom in Canada West. The ports of Sandusky, Huron, Lorain, Conneaut, Cleveland, Painesville and Ashtabula in Ohio, as well as Oswego, Pultneyville and Rochester in New York, were disembarkation points.[40]

Generally, three major arteries developed. In the East, fugitives from slavery traveled up through Virginia, Maryland and Delaware to Lancaster and Chester Counties in Pennsylvania, where they were sent to Philadelphia and New York City or up through eastern or central Pennsylvania. In either case, they could be sent farther north to upstate New York and eventually to Suspension Bridge, not far from Niagara Falls, to cross into Canada. Other times they were sent by ship from the Virginia ports to New York City or New England seaports like New Bedford. Fugitives also were sent from the District of Columbia, where Charles T. Torrey and Thomas Smallwood organized its UGRR network in 1842.[41]

In the west (today the Midwest), that river of freedom, the Ohio, had important crossing points at Evansville, New Albany and Madison, Indiana; at Cincinnati, Ripley, Portsmouth and Marietta, Ohio; at Louisville and Maysville, Kentucky; and at Wheeling, Virginia. Both Indiana and Ohio had hundreds of Underground stations, most of them conducted by Quakers, Baptists, New School Presbyterians and free people of color.

Farther west, the route was first developed by Reverend John Cross in the early 1840s. It led mainly from Quincy, Illinois, through Galesburg, Princeton, Chicago and southern Michigan, ending in Detroit. This route extended across Iowa and into Kansas by 1854 and had some traffic coming through St. Louis and Alton, Illinois.[42]

After 1850, with the surge in the development of rail travel, the "upperground" railroad was increasingly used.[43] It covered a lot of territory. From Maine to Kansas, from below the Mason-Dixon in the District of Columbia and even into the Deep South along the Mississippi River. There riverboat hands (like Springfield, Ohio's Henry Roberts) who had deep conviction and good hearts aided those in slavery to escape.[44]

The UGRR was widespread and diversified. In the large urban areas like Philadelphia, New York, Boston and Detroit, there were well-organized vigilance committees. In communities like West Chester County, Pennsylvania, or smaller cities like Harrisburg, Pennsylvania, or Albany, Syracuse and Rochester, New York, there were tightly knit groups that were in close contact with the larger vigilance committees. In western states like Ohio, Michigan, Indiana and Illinois, it was more decentralized and localized. But these descriptions are not rigid because the UGRR was, by necessity, improvisational. A truly integrated movement, it included individuals from all walks of life, all races and genders—even, on rare occasions, slaveholders themselves—all with one compassionate purpose: "to help the oppressed go free."

Chapter 3

THE LEGACY OF WILBUR SIEBERT AND HIS UNDERGROUND RAILROAD

I t's probably not a coincidence that the UGRR's most important historian lived near its epicenter. Wilbur Siebert was born in 1866 in Columbus, went to Ohio State and received his master's in history from Harvard. Subsequently, he studied history and philosophy at the universities of Freiberg and Berlin in Germany. He returned in 1891 to a position as a professor at Ohio State, where he remained throughout his long career. His interest in the UGRR began almost immediately when students told him stories about their families' involvement. It led to the distribution of his "circular" that began in 1892 and contained seven questions inquiring about the who-what-where of the UGRR.[45] This circular was passed around like a chain letter and spread throughout the states north of the Mason-Dixon line. In 1894 and 1895, he went to Ontario (Canada West) to interview those who had been fugitive slaves and who had settled there. After some years, the responses to his circular numbered in the thousands. His seminal work, *The Underground Railroad: From Slavery to Freedom*, published in 1898, was drawn in part from the responses he received. He also incorporated all of the earlier important sources, notably the books by William Still, Levi Coffin and Robert Smedley, all of which were based on the experiences of those who participated, as well as the county histories that were published throughout the United States in the nineteenth century and that contain a wealth of local history.

Wilbur Siebert. *Courtesy Ohio History Center.*

In the preface to this book, Siebert wrote the following about his method:

> *This volume is the outgrowth of an investigation begun in 1892–1893, when the writer was giving a portion of his time to the teaching of United States history in the Ohio State University. The search for materials was carried on at intervals during several years until the mass of information, written and printed, was deemed sufficient to be subjected to the processes of analysis and generalization.*
>
> *Patience and care have been required to overcome the difficulties attaching to a subject that was in an extraordinary sense a hidden one; and the author has constantly tried to observe those well-known dicta of the historian; namely, to be content with the materials discovered without making additions of his own, and to let his conclusions be defined by the facts, rather than seek to cast these "in the mould of his hypothesis."*[46]

In later years, Siebert used the same method to write books about the UGRR in Massachusetts, Vermont and, finally, his last book, Ohio. Today, the Siebert Collection—which also includes news clippings, dissertations of students who used and analyzed his work and other documents—is housed at the Ohio History Connection in Columbus and at Harvard University. A digital copy also is available online at OhioMemory.org. However, his work has lost favor with serious historians. You might say that a blight has developed on his portrayal of the UGRR.

How did this happen? Probably it relates to our tendency to mythologize what or whom we admire. Heroes often become legendary; some even take on that quality in their own time. Events, too, seem of greater import when viewed in retrospect, with nostalgic emotion. We all do it; we all remember the good old days. And so it was with the UGRR. No one can argue that selflessly helping others in need, sometimes to the point of self-sacrifice, as with the UGRR, is not human behavior at its highest good. It was only natural that it would become mythic and legendary.

One of the legends associated with the UGRR was its secrecy, precisely because it was illegal to help those escaping slavery. This secrecy engendered a fascination with hiding places, which sometimes were described in accounts of those who aided fugitives from slavery. It made perfect sense. But it also led to false expectations, to a belief that every small nook or cranny in an old house, of which there were many, or that every old well or tunnel used in farming or some other utilitarian purpose may have been used as part of the UGRR. These beliefs were never promoted by Siebert.

Historian Larry Gara looked askance at some of these claims and decided that not only did they need some reasonable scrutiny but also that there were other shortcomings in the classic portrayal that needed to be rectified. His 1961 book, *Liberty Line*, was his answer. He came to three important conclusions:

- *The number of Underground Railroad passengers was vastly exaggerated.*
- *There was little organization in regard to the Underground Railroad and the work was mainly conducted by blacks; the role of whites was inflated by propaganda and self-promotion.*
- *The part fugitive slaves played in their escape has been vastly underemphasized.*[47]

Gara was right when he said the abolitionist newspapers fueled the fire of the abolitionist movement. William Lloyd Garrison was not about to move a "single inch," as he proclaimed in the first issue of *The Liberator* and which actually occurred in 1834 when he faced a mob that actually led him through the streets of Boston with a noose around his neck. Gara was more right than he realized. As pointed out earlier in the first chapter, the antislavery newspapers were often the hubs for the UGRR—their offices often harboring fugitives and being the meeting places of vigilance committees.[48] A little hyperbole goes a long way, but that doesn't mean the UGRR didn't help many thousands.

Gara's revisionist view of the UGRR also came at a propitious time, during the bloom of the Civil Rights movement. The heroics of the UGRR, whose traditional view had focused mainly on whites, were shifted to people of color. His reasoning made sense and was justified by the facts. Black history from that period had mainly been preserved by oral tradition, as most slaves were never taught to read or write, and this resulted in a paucity of memoirs by them. This is true to some degree, although there were many eloquent people of color from that period, most notably Frederick Douglass, one of the greatest writers of the nineteenth century, and William Still, who wrote one of the most important and detailed books about the UGRR in which he played a leading role.

He is probably right about numbers—they were exaggerated. Most people were just making guestimates. Round numbers like one, two or three thousand are often attributed to various individuals. Few kept track; only those like Levi Coffin, whose traffic was regular for so many years, and Thomas Garrett, who actually kept track for most of his three-plus decades, can give us reasonably accurate numbers, and they were probably the two

Left: William Lloyd Garrison. *Library of Congress*.

Right: Frederick Douglass.

most active agents in the history of the UGRR. Canadian census records, where the overwhelming majority of people of color listed were American fugitives, record far lower numbers[49] than would be expected if all the claims of individuals were added up. Robin Winks, whose work *The Blacks in Canada* is the authoritative source, does note that apparently many people of color were constantly moving back and forth to Canada at that time, so actual numbers are difficult to estimate.[50] Nevertheless, with many fugitives in hiding in the North, to say that twenty thousand fugitives had escaped over the years is a conservative estimate, and it is reasonable to put the figure on the other side of thirty thousand. Still, a considerable accomplishment.

Where the Gara version erred was taking all the credit away from the white abolitionists, who gave totally without receiving, and attributing much more of the escaping to the pluck and fortitude of the fugitive. Running into the wilderness, sometimes without much knowledge of what lay, ahead was a formidable task. To think that even extraordinary individuals would not need help considering the additional deterrent of nightly slave patrols on horseback running with their "Negro dogs," which were trained to attack people of color, is ridiculous. Everyone needs help in such situations, and luck. It does not make sense for the fugitives to go it totally alone when there were so many people ready and willing to help them once they crossed into a free state.[51]

"Negro dogs." *Library of Congress.*

The final chapter of *Liberty Line* is perhaps its most controversial and arguably the one that has had the most lasting influence. In "Reminiscence and Romance," Gara wrote, "Seldom do historians accept the reminiscences of aged participants without the careful evaluation of such material," an obvious reference to the work of Siebert, which depended so heavily on "such material." It seems he missed what Siebert had to say about it, anticipating such an argument, which is as follows:

> [I]t may be said that a large part of the materials for this history were drawn from written and oral accounts obtained at a much later date; and that these materials, even though the honesty and fidelity of the narrators be granted, are worthy of little credit for historical purposes. [But] It would be difficult to imagine an "old-time" abolitionist, whose faculties are in a fair state of preservation, forgetting that he received fugitives from a certain neighbor or community a few miles away, that he usually stowed them in his garret or his haymow, and that he was in the habit of taking them at night in all kinds of weather to one of several different stations, the managers of which he knew intimately and trusted implicitly…the strange and romantic character of his unlawful business helped to fix them in his mind…because they were in some way extraordinary…it should not be forgotten that it is a fact of common observation that old persons ordinarily remember the occurrences of their youth and prime better than events of recent date…. The risks these persons ran…the disdain of the communities where they lived, have secured to us a source of knowledge…which cannot be lightly questioned. If there be doubt on this point, it must give way before…the testimony of different and sometimes widely separated witnesses combining to support one another.[52]

What really is compelling about Siebert's statement is that so many of the accounts corroborate one another, although often the respondents had either moved far away or had lost complete touch with the person who would corroborate what they said.

A prominent contemporary historian seized on Gara's take that the accounts Siebert collected were less than accurate and extremely hyperbolic. This historian's writings on historical memory have led to new interpretations of the causes of the Civil War, and rightly so. But when he tried to apply the same theory to the UGRR, he failed miserably.

"Some Northerners were attracted to yet other mythologies," he wrote. "Such was the crusade of the 1890s, led by an Ohio university professor, to collect the lore of the UGRR." He called Siebert's method of assembling the recollections "sentimental retrospection" and invented the notion that the respondents were "eager to claim their places...in a heroic legacy, as veterans of the 'old liberty life guard.'" He goes on, with more purple prose: "Many of those who answered the professor's call were seeking what we might call an alternative veteranhood....As in soldiers' battle narratives, alleged UGRR operatives recited their battles with slave catchers, and they remembered virtually no defeats."[53]

This sarcasm is no more credible than a hidey-hole at the Canadian border in northern New York or Vermont. On the other hand, such a hiding place is conceivable if unlikely considering that it was an illegal business and there were many in the North who were proslavery.[54]

Nevertheless, this revisionist view has become dogma in the academic community. An op-ed in the *New York Times* in 2015 by two academics described it. They said where Siebert went wrong was in accepting the accounts he collected at "face value," a phrase used by Gara. They also said that the accounts used by Siebert were those of "mainly white" abolitionists, tinging his portrayal. They erroneously claimed that postbellum literature conjured up a view that the UGRR operated in "every town north of the Mason-Dixon Line" and wrote that the reality was that "most fugitive slaves gained their freedom largely through their own efforts."

Apparently, these academics had not considered the obstacles of fleeing on foot unaided through what was then mostly wilderness. But thousands did manage to successfully escape. Finally, they belittled the efforts of the abolitionists whose stories comprised Siebert's UGRR as "self-serving," a "way to bask in the glory of the cause," something that recalls the prominent historian.[55] They questioned Siebert's method, calling his reliance on his collection "a specious defense of these sources,"[56] much like the prominent historian who called it "a dubious theory of memory."[57] To give truth to power, so to speak, this prominent historian had cited an example that perfectly fit his theory of historical memory. He referenced a "nostalgic" newspaper account from the Marysville, Ohio *Tribune*, dated September 29, 1897, that told the story of the "'fearless and uncompromising abolitionist,' Udney H. Hyde." He wrote that this story "struck a chord…so deep that it is sometimes difficult to separate truly heroic abolitionism from romantic adventure stories."[58] But this romantic adventure story had verification that went far beyond an 1897 reminiscence. It was a story that had actually reached the pages of the *New York Tribune* in 1857 and had literally more than one hundred accounts in the daily and weekly newspapers of that time throughout the state of Ohio.[59] It is the story that was told in part in chapter 1, based on these accounts. It's a wonder how the prominent historian missed it.

Certainly, memory fades over time. This is why we record our history, to preserve it, to leave a lasting imprint of our presence and to provide lessons for those who come after us. Historians who neglect the use of statements by those who gain nothing by untruth cease to become true historians and merely purveyors of propaganda to serve their personal prejudices. The story of the UGRR is a real one, contemporary documents corroborate this and the words of those who provided their recollections to Siebert were not people making up stories. While it was illegal and people did try to conceal their activities, there are mountains of evidence showing that it was much more than legendary.

Chapter 4

THE CONUNDRUM OF COLOR

W hy color? Is it as elemental as day and night? What in our psyche has caused this prejudice against the darker shade of skin? Certainly slavery based on skin color being a part of America, more than one hundred years before there was a United States, had a role. But there is no simple answer. The fact remains and continues even today, if perhaps to a lesser degree.

In Ohio it was evident, despite the Northwest Ordinance of 1787 that prohibited slavery in the Northwest Territories. The Black Laws imposed in 1804 only ten months after it became a state illustrated the feeling of the electorate that people of color were not wanted.

The 1800 census showed only 337 free people of color, yet the state enacted the Black Law of 1804 that required all those of color to post a $500 bond ($7,500 in today's dollars) just so that they could live there, and anyone who employed them without a certificate of freedom would be fined and required to make restitution to the "owner."

The 1807 additions to the law prohibited African Americans from testifying in court proceedings in which whites were involved and made it illegal to hire an African American who did not have a certificate of freedom. Later, when the public school system in Ohio was established in 1829, there was no provision for black children. African Americans also could not serve on juries, vote or join the militia.

To say that people of color in antebellum Ohio were much less than free is surely an understatement, and in many sections of the state, they were not even welcome. However, because of the small numbers of blacks in the state during the early part of the nineteenth century, the Black Laws fell into disuse. As their population increased, a movement arose to change that. In Cincinnati, it was decided in 1829 to strongly enforce the state's Black Laws, which up to that time had been neglected. This was probably because of the growing population of people of color in the city, which had reached more than three thousand when one takes into account the number of fugitives from slavery hiding there.[60] In fact, a petition had been presented to the city government by whites to put a halt to this growth.[61]

Despite announcements in the newspapers demanding compliance with the Black Laws, there was resistance. Finally, on August 15, tensions exploded and mobs of whites "attacked and demolished" the homes of blacks and went on violent spree that lasted about a week. Both sides suffered injuries, although only one death was reported, that of a white man. The riot ended, but it drove out more than half of the city's black population."[62] Some went to Canada, where they formed the first black settlement of American emigrants, naming it Wilberforce, after the renowned English abolitionist.

A similar event occurred several months later in Portsmouth, Ohio, about one hundred miles east of Cincinnati, where the entire black population of about eighty residents were driven out of town without even being allowed to take their possessions—all for not complying with the Black Laws.[63]

There were other such responses around the state, including a move in 1846 to prevent the relocation of the newly freed slaves of John Randolph of Roanoke, Virginia, to Mercer County, where some blacks had been settled by abolitionist Augustus Wattles in 1835.[64] As Ohio historian Caleb Atwater wrote in 1838:

> [I]t is [in] our interest…to have slavery continued in the slave holding states, for a century yet, otherwise our growth would be checked…the streams of wealth…now rolling into Ohio would be stayed, and would be rolled back to their sources, rendering those states our superiors…..No, we have adopted a policy which for a century yet requires slavery in the states south of us to be continued.[65]

It's a wonder people of color would actually settle in Ohio. Yet they came. Why? One reason was that they were mostly newly freed slaves from Virginia, and according to state law, they were required to move out of the state. One of the first and the largest was the Gist settlement.

Samuel Gist was an absentee landlord of plantations in Virginia. Formerly an indentured servant in America, he gained his wealth by marrying the widow of his master. Being a Loyalist, he moved back to England during the early signs of the American Revolution. He owned several plantations in Virginia on which perhaps as many as one thousand slaves lived and had others manage them. In 1808, he decided to free all his slaves at the time of his death. But he wasn't merely freeing them to live on their own. He also was purchasing land, building them homes and providing schools and churches. In addition, all taxes on the lands would be paid. It was his intention to care for them for the remainder of their lives with the hope that eventually they would become self-sufficient. This project was put into a trust that was to be managed by prominent Virginia lawyer John Wickham.

In 1815, Gist died at the age of ninety-two. After his death, Wickham turned over the management of the trust to his son, William. After some legal maneuvering, William chose Ohio as the place where he would move the newly freed slaves. While William managed the financial matters, he chose three Quakers to act as agents in organizing the settlement. Settlements were organized first in Brown County, Ohio, in 1819 and 1821 and in Highland County, Ohio, in 1832 and involved several hundred freed slaves—good choices considering that antislavery had already taken hold there.

However, many problems arose regarding the quality of the land, difficulties in providing adequate education and its overall finances. *The History of Brown County* described their predicament:

> *Here…came nearly 900 persons, a part of whom located on the Georgetown lands, the remainder on the Fincastle purchase. Their "comfortable homes" lay in the wild region about them; the education they received was in the stern school of adversity. As a matter of course, they did not prosper.*[66]

It turned out that one of the agents, Joshua Woodrow, had embezzled money from the trust. In addition, the residents of the settlements were never given the titles to the deeded property, which caused a host of problems that continue for some even today. In addition, despite the strong antislavery sentiment in the area, there were still many who were racist. Hostile attitudes of neighbors were prevalent despite the efforts of neighboring Quakers, who contributed money and aid to them.[67]

The importance of the settlements to the UGRR was that they were natural shelters for fugitives from slavery. How much is still uncertain, and it comes mainly from oral tradition. John Hudson, for example, was singled out by UGRR manager Isaac Beck of Sardinia as his best conductor:

> [Among those] *who engaged in the operations here* [was] *the man who guided more than any other was John D. Hudson, one of the Gist slaves, a boy when he came here and by his exertions obtained an education as good as our common laborers (There were no free schools for darkies), a man of good intellect and powerful physique and when enraged, no more fear than a mad bull. He was poor and we contributed and paid him wages for the time he was thus engaged. I paid him twenty-five cents a trip for my share* [five dollars in today's money]. *The mode of travel was sometimes afoot, sometimes on horses, sometimes in wagons and the route chosen was governed by the circumstances of each case.*[68]

While the Gist settlements were not successful in raising the status of people of color, there were other smaller settlements started by free blacks who had moved from Virginia into southern Ohio. They were located eastward and were very active in the UGRR. They included the settlements of Poke Patch, Gallia County; Ironton, Lawrence County; and Berlin Crossroads, Jackson County.

The Poke Patch–Ironton line had an interesting confluence of factors. An insightful and detailed study of Poke Patch and its relationship to the UGRR was done by Cheryl LaRoche. But even more convincing testament to its UGRR history is a man of color who actually manned it, Gabe N. Johnson:[69]

> *I was born in Spotsylvania County, Virginia, in 1824…raised in Burlington* [Lawrence County, Ohio] *and worked along the river front.*
>
> *The Underground work began under my immediate observation in 1846.…I was* [a] *barber in the Madison House in Cincinnati.…* [And] *I got into the work* [there].…*Coffin was the main man.*[70] *The fugitives were taken to Mt. Auburn, then to a place west of Hamilton.…I worked the UGRR in Cincinnati till '54 or '55.*[71] *I was the first man that established anything like a systematized road here in Ironton: I and…James Dicher* [also spelled "Ditcher" by Johnson], *a colored man from Pennsylvania. He would take more chances for his life than any man I ever saw.*
>
> [The fugitives] *used to cross the river at Guyandotte.…Philip Lynch (colored), and Rev. Beaman—a white Presbyterian preacher were in it*

with me there. [Also] *there was John Campbell—he and I had made those woods when the snow was foot deep.*

John S. Stewart and Eliza, his wife [of Poke Patch, originally called the Stewart Settlement], *were…ardent workers* [in the UGRR]. *There were five Stewart brothers: T.N., James W., Isaac, John S., and Jacob.* [They] *were all active workers. Their parents came from Virginia, and were free born.…Jacob was the leading spirit. John Matthews, colored, who lived in Olive Furnace—about five miles from Poke Patch was also an efficient worker.*

The first runaway…passed through in 1844. His name was Wilson and he came from Virginia. Her husband…piloted him to Berlin Crossroads, a place where a large number of free colored people had settled… [and] *generally piloted the fugitive slaves to the house of Noah Nooks.*

There were others, and in all, about two hundred fugitives passed through Poke Patch, about half of them aided by the Stewart family. But according to Johnson, it was only one of the destinations used by Dicher, whom he described as a "tall, thin man with an Indian complexion…called the 'red fox' who resorted to many trick and ruses to throw the…human bloodhounds off the scent of their human prey."

What is often overlooked by historians are the logistics involved in the UGRR. An indispensable cog in this area's UGRR was the previously mentioned John Campbell. The founder of Ironton in 1840, he helped build eleven of the area's many blast furnaces and was part owner in eight of them. His business, which served the area's burgeoning iron industry in that area, hired many free people of color who had moved to the area.[72] Some, like John Stewart, whom he appointed as an iron master, were involved in the UGRR. He also supplied the horses and the wagons used to transport the fugitives north, building a large barn in Ironton where horses and wagons were stabled and where fugitives were hidden.[73]

LaRoche's study also links several small black Baptist churches in the area to the UGRR. One of them, the Union Baptist Church, was organized in 1819 and formed the Providence Anti-Slavery Missionary Baptist Association in 1821. This church, which served Poke Patch, was located in Black Fork, an iron company town founded by the Washington Iron Furnace Company, with which Campbell also was associated.[74]

Interestingly, Campbell was not the only iron entrepreneur in the region who may have had ties to the UGRR. John Means moved from South Carolina to nearby Hanging Rock and freed and brought his slaves. In 1826, he established the Union Furnace. No records show his involvement in the UGRR, but he certainly brought potential workers for it.[75]

This connection between the iron industry in southern Ohio and the black community is a classic example of the integrated effort of the UGRR. Logistics are very important: money for food, clothing and transportation were essential. Debunkers of the UGRR would have you believe that random individuals with passionate beliefs were all that comprised the UGRR. This is preposterous. No wonder they think it was exaggerated. Such lack of cooperation and organization would have been very unsuccessful. And we know that isn't true, or the South wouldn't have pushed so strongly for the passage of the FSL of 1850.

Berlin Crossroads, the next important stop on the line, was significant for another reason: it spawned a powerful leader of the black community, one who has been called the father of "Black Nationalism." His father, Reverend Thomas C. Woodson, was its founder. His descendants claim him to have been the first child of Thomas Jefferson and Sally Hemings.[76] Woodson had been a slave in a Virginia plantation near Monticello and would have been about the age when records indicate that Hemings had a child named Tom who allegedly died soon afterward.[77]

Woodson and his wife, Jemima, moved to Chillicothe, Ohio, in 1820 and were founding members of its Quinn Chapel African Methodist Episcopal (AME) Church. As early as 1821, their eldest son, Lewis, only twenty at the time, is alleged to have retrieved a fugitive who had been kidnapped from Chillicothe. But Chillicothe was a proslavery town, settled by former slave owners who bought land through grants from the Virginia Military District. In 1829, the family founded Berlins Crossroads, where they continued their involvement, according to oral tradition,[78] and spawned a network in Jackson County of black conductors. Wilson Hawk, a Berlin Cross Roads resident, described it:

> *I know that it went on early while I was a boy for I heard it spoken of from time to time. The colored folks lived all around us and I was well acquainted with many of them.*
>
> *A great many times the colored folks, would come out of Virginia. Sometimes out of Kentucky, run away principally themselves and come here. Along in the fifties there was heaps of it.*
>
> *Noah Nooks, a colored man was the principal one in it here. They principally tarried at his house one fourth of a mile or so from here, just outside of the town where he owned, a farm of 160 acres…*

Some walked and some rode through the hills and they were delivered to a white man generally at Wilkesvile. Abraham Morris. In that neighborhood there was a number concerned but Morris was the principal one.[79]

An 1838 article in the *Colored American* discussed the success of the Woodson settlement.

Six miles from Jackson…there are between 20 and 30 colored families who came from Virginia. I think there is not a family in the settlement, the head, or entire body of which, has not been the legal property of Virginia merchants. Most of them were the children, as well as the slaves of their masters; and were emancipated by them. Some, however, purchased themselves. The inhabitants are farmers, with two or three exceptions, who are mechanics. All of them own…property, and some…are wealthy. Thomas Woodson was the son of his master, and his wife the daughter of hers. He purchased himself and family for $900. He came to this State several years ago, and when he arrived here he was almost penniless. He now owns 372 acres of good land, acknowledged to be the best cultivated farm in Jackson county. Sometimes fifty stacks of hay may be seen on his farm in one season. He raises annually from 1500-to-3000 bushels of corn. I have never found a more intelligent, enterprising, farming family in the state of Ohio.[80]

Oral tradition claims that two sons of the Woodson family, Thomas and John P, both ministers of the AME Church who were active in the UGRR, died at the hands of proslavery mobs.[81]

Emerging from the Woodson family as a militant, national leader among blacks in the antislavery movement was Lewis, a minister in the AME Church who moved to Pittsburgh. He was active in the Black Conventions of the day and involved in many social causes. He was among the strongest advocates for black self-determination and urged blacks to become farmers and live away from the urban areas as a way to escape the prejudice of white society.

In a letter to the *Colored American*, he wrote:

Our people have shown a disposition adverse to settling in the country. They have heretofore been in the habit of crowding into the large towns and cities, and settling there, for no other reason, of which I can conceive, than the enjoyment of each other's society…

A more powerful means of changing our present dependent and precarious condition, into one of comfort and independence, could be devised…settling in the country and becoming the owners and cultivators of the soil. The possession of houses and lands, and flocks and herds, inspires the possessor with a nobleness and independence, unknown to those in any other business. Everything by which he is surrounded tends to the preservation of his morals, and the integrity and elevation of his soul.[82]

Probably the most important man of color to be nurtured in the soil of antebellum Ohio was John Mercer Langston, the first African American to be elected to Congress in 1893 following the period of Black Reconstruction in the South that lasted until 1876, when former Confederates were not allowed to vote.[83]

Although Langston was elected in the state of Virginia, the place of his birth, he spent most of his formative years and adult life in Ohio. Born a slave in 1829 on a Louisa County, Virginia plantation, like Box Brown, he was the son of his master, Ralph Quarles. Embodying the qualities of the so-called benevolent slaveholder, Quarles openly claimed John and his older brothers Gideon and Charles, and half brother William, as his own. He employed no overseers and believed that slavery should be abolished, but voluntarily by each slaveholder. "He held that slaves should be dealt with… [so] as to prevent cruelty…and to inspire in them…feelings of confidence in their master."[84]

John was only four when both his father and mother, Lucy Langston, who was part Native American and black, died in 1834. His father left him and his brothers an ample inheritance, which they were not permitted to claim until reaching the age of twenty-one. Because laws required newly freed slaves to leave Virginia, it was decided that the boys would be sent to Ohio. They took the surname of their mother, and Gideon, who was twenty-one, took responsibility for Charles, then sixteen. Quarles's close friend Colonel John Gooch, who lived in Chillicothe, became John's guardian. Gooch's eldest daughter taught him how to read and write, and he said it was five of the happiest years of his life. Meanwhile, Gooch helped Gideon and Charles enroll at the Preparatory Academy (high school) at Oberlin.

After five years, Gooch was offered a business opportunity in Missouri. John could have moved with him, but his older half brother, William, thought it better that he stay in Ohio and entrusted him to New England abolitionist Richard Long, who had bought the Gooch farm. Long sent him to the Baker Street Baptist Church, where he boarded with John Woodson, a black activist and superintendent of the AME Church's Sunday school.[85] In his autobiography, Langston vividly described the Cincinnati Riot against blacks in 1841. Later, he moved in with black entrepreneur William W. Watson, a former slave and barber. He, too, was a Sunday school superintendent, but of the Baker Street Baptist Church, which was known as the "headquarters of Cincinnati's Underground Railroad."[86]

In 1844, John enrolled at the preparatory academy in Oberlin. Here was where he would grow into one of the great black orators of his time and begin his legal career. After completing studies at the preparatory academy, he entered the college, majoring in theology. There he came under the influence of perhaps the greatest evangelist of that era, Reverend Charles Grandison Finney, head of the Theology Department, who later became Oberlin College's president from 1851 to 1866.

So quickly did John advance that in 1850, he joined Frederick Douglass on a lecture tour through the Midwest. After the passage of the second fugitive slave law in September 1850, he joined his brother, Charles, in the antislavery crusade and helped to organize the Young Men's Anti-Slavery Society of Oberlin. Fugitive slaves regularly came to the village, and a special school was established for them.[87]

Langston set his sights on a law career. There were few African American lawyers and none in Ohio. Despite impressive credentials, his applications to law school were rejected. Consequently, he continued his studies in theology, thinking that it would help prepare him for law. After earning a master's degree, he found employment with the law firm of Philemon Bliss in nearby Elyria, which helped prepare him for the bar exam. In the spring of 1855, he became Brownhelm town clerk, the first black elected to public office in America. As town clerk, he was responsible for legal and financial matters. The latter involved funds put aside to aid fugitives from slavery.

Not everyone was pleased with Langston's political ascent. The previous clerk was angered over his loss to a black man. He began a campaign of agitation against the town by collaborating with slave catchers in the rendition of fugitive slaves. In September 1858, the slave catchers met success with the abduction of John Price, a fugitive slave from Kentucky. They proceeded with him to Wellington, a village about ten miles south of Oberlin, awaiting the next train to Columbus, Ohio, at the Wadsworth House hotel.

The people of Oberlin wasted little time in tracking them down. Acting as spokesman for the armed posse, numbering as many as five hundred, was none other than John's brother, Charles. They surrounded the hotel, and Charles demanded Price's release. When the slave catchers refused, they took Price by force. Thirty-seven of the Oberlin-Wellington rescuers were prosecuted and refused bail, spending eighty-three days

John Mercer Langston. *Library of Congress.*

in jail awaiting their trial. One of two men convicted was Charles, who spent twenty days in jail.

As the Civil War approached, Langston was among those advocating ending slavery by force. Two men who went with John Brown to Harpers Ferry were recruited by the Langston: Sheridan Leary, who died during the assault, and John Copeland, also one of the thirty-seven Oberlin-Wellington rescuers, who was hanged two weeks after Brown. During the Civil War, Langston worked to recruit black troops. George Stearns, one of John Brown's chief financial supporters, chose him to recruit men in the west for the Massachusetts Fifty-Fourth Regiment.

After the war, Langston was selected to work with the freedmen as inspector of the Bureau of Refugees, Freedmen and Abandoned Lands. He helped his supervisor, General Oliver Otis Howard, establish Howard University and for nine years served as its law school dean. An appointment as ambassador to Haiti, which he held for eight more years, led up to his successful election to Congress.

A particularly moving experience for him came during the Civil War in January 1865. African Americans had by then entered the Union army in full force, and he was asked to speak to the many freedmen encamping in areas taken by the Union army in Nashville, Tennessee, to boost their morale. Following his pep talk, a powerfully built, white-haired corporal suddenly called him by name.

"John," he called out, surprising Langston, who slowly approached him. "John, I held you in the hollow of this hand. I'm from Louisa County." Langston was astonished, for the man was obviously well into his fifties. "I had to get into this fight until there is no more slavery in the land."

"You were a slave?" Langston asked.

"Always a slave, John. But always a fugitive slave, always a fugitive slave."[88]

Langston retired to his homestead in Petersburg, Virginia, following his term in Congress and died in Washington, D.C., in 1897. His upbringing in the hotbed of Ohio abolition and its constant struggles with slave catchers to free fugitives from slavery prepared him to go where other black men had not yet gone.

Chapter 5

THE OASIS OF BENEVOLENCE

T he roots of antislavery and the UGRR in Ohio stem from Brown County and Ripley, Ohio, and branch out through the rest of the state. While another root was planted in southeast Ohio, the first calls for immediate emancipation did not come, as is generally believed, from Quaker Charles Osborne, who had settled there after the formation in 1814 of his Tennessee Manumission Society. They came twenty years earlier with evangelists who had settled in Brown County.

Quakers were not the only source of antislavery sentiment. Presbyterians, Baptists and Methodists whose antislavery beliefs had developed as a result of the Second Great Awakening were speaking out in the rural settlements of Kentucky, Tennessee and western Virginia. It was a resumption of the First Great Awakening in America, which had begun around 1730 and offered the promise of salvation to all who abandoned their sinful ways and followed the doctrine of Christ—to do good works for others as it would be done for them. The second Awakening differed in that it appealed to the common man. The earlier emphasis in American Christianity had been on the Calvinist ethic, which stated that a person's success in life was a sign that they were among those chosen by God. Being poor or unsuccessful showed that they had been tainted by sin.[89]

In the frontier hamlets, self-reliant individuals interacted on equal footing with one another, and status was unimportant. This egalitarian ideal needed a religious faith to serve that vision. It prompted the eruption of religious happenings called revivals, where hundreds and sometimes thousands of people gathered to hear preachers, often of competing denominations, calling on them to repent their sins and seek salvation as followers of Jesus Christ. Its earliest surge occurred from 1798 to 1810 in Kentucky, where camp meeting revivals drew as many as twenty-five thousand persons. According to *The History of the Chillicothe Presbytery* by Reverend R.C. Galbraith, published in 1889, "It affected all the regions whence the settlers of Southern and Central Ohio were drawn."[90] This is important for our understanding of the fervor for antislavery that was developed in this forsaken part of the UGRR.

What was described seems beyond the realm of our present belief. It gives insight into the zeal that motivated those involved in the UGRR. Galbraith quoted a book written in 1808 by Richard McNemar, one of the synod's early members, in describing it:

> *The meetings were always held in the forest near some church, which furnished a lodging place for the preachers. As the meetings progressed and the excitement grew more intense, and the crowd rushed from preacher to preacher, singing, shouting, laughing, calling upon men to repent, men and women fell upon the ground unable to help themselves, and in such numbers that it was impossible for the multitude to move about, especially at night, when the excitement was greatest….As time passed on and the meetings grew more frequent, even stranger forms of this intense nervous excitement appeared. One of these was known as jerking* [also referred to as "the jerks"]. *It is said that at camp meetings in the far South…Men dreamed dreams and saw visions—nay, fancied themselves dogs, went down on all fours, and barked till they grew hoarse. It was no uncommon sight to behold numbers of them gathered about a tree, barking, yelping, "treeing the devil."*[91]

This revival experience touched not only Kentucky and Ohio but also nearly every rural hamlet in America. It furthered the development of the circuit rider, the itinerant preacher who traveled hundreds of miles weekly on horseback, scouring the countryside for lost souls to bring the gospel of salvation. It was the circuit rider who served as the model for the abolitionist lecturers,[92] and what makes it so crucial to the development of antislavery in the forsaken region is that the formative years of its early progenitors occurred during this Awakening.

One of these pioneers of immediate abolition was Brown County Presbyterian Reverend James Gilliland. A native of South Carolina, he was reprimanded by the Presbytery of South Carolina for preaching against slavery in 1796. He obeyed its command until he could no longer keep silent, and in 1805, he took the pastorate in Red Oak, Ohio, five miles north of Ripley, where he preached for the next thirty-nine years. "The Rev. Mr. Gilliland…often preached abolition and always 'immediatism'…and [that] fact would be testified by every old resident."[93] He was acknowledged as the leading abolition spokesman in the Ripley area and the father of four other abolitionist churches in the county, Russellville, Decatur, Georgetown and Ripley, where John Rankin became pastor in 1821. Rankin was already an immediatist when he came to Ohio, having been a member of Osborne's society in Tennessee. Gilliland and Rankin became frequent collaborators in the UGRR, with Rankin's sons being regulars at his stop.[94]

It is claimed that as many as one thousand fugitives from slavery were aided through this area of Presbyterian evangelism before 1817.[95] Giving this credence was a complaint that year by the Kentucky legislature to the State of Ohio that fugitive slaves were crossing into Ohio and that the state was doing nothing to prevent it.[96] This was during a time when the population was sparse and the roads few and primitive. The Mississippi River was the far west, and Ohio was still much like a wilderness. It was said that these early fugitives followed on foot the trails of the Bullskin Trace near present-day Route 133, which had been carved out by long-since-vanished buffalo herds, and the Mound Builder trails that began near Manchester.[97]

Joining Gilliland and Rankin as cogs in the UGRR were fellow Presbyterians Dr. Alexander Campbell and William Dunlop of Ripley. Among their

ABOLITION SOCIETY OF PAINT VALLEY.

Agreeably to adjournment, the Abolition Society of Paint Valley, Ohio, held its annual meeting, on Wednesday, the 28th of August, 1833, and the following officers were chosen.

GEORGE BROWN, Esq. *President.*
WILLIAM WILSON, Esq. *V. President.*
ADAM B. WILSON, Esq. *Rec. Sec'ry.*
Rev. JAMES H. DICKEY, *Cor. Sec'ry.*
Mr. JOSEPH LAWHEAD, *Treasurer.*

Members of the Executive Committee for Highland County.
Rev. SAMUEL CROTHERS,
Hon. HUGH SMART.

For Fayette County.
Mr. HUGH GHORMLY,
Mr. JAMES McCONNEL.

For Ross County.
WILLIAM SMITH, Esq.
Mr. JAMES C. STEELE.

The Liberator, October 12, 1833.

colleagues in the Chillicothe Presbytery were Reverend Jesse Lockhart of Russellville; Reverend Samuel Crothers of Greenfield; Reverend William Dickey of Bloomingburg; William's brother, James, and Hugh S. Fullerton in Ross County; and Reverend Dyer Burgess in Adams County, all of whom aided fugitives from slavery.

One can only speculate the influence that this synod had on this area, but suffice it to say, in 1835, the year the Ohio Anti-Slavery Society was organized, the Paint Valley Anti-Slavery Society formed by residents of Highland, Fayette and Ross Counties listed 942 members, by far the largest in the state.

The writings of Rankin and Crothers were influential. On December 2, 1823, Rankin's brother, Thomas, in Virginia wrote to him that he had purchased a slave. It deeply troubled him, and he began a series of letters, fifteen in all, explaining why slavery was sinful. The following comes from "Letter Thirteen":

> *There is no divine permission for enslaving the Africans, and therefore the command is as obligatory upon their enslavers as it was upon the emancipating Israelites. Hence, every slaveholder is commanded to break the yoke of bondage, and "To let the oppressed go free."*
>
> *Every man who is acquainted with the attendant and consequent evils of slavery would, if a slave, desire to be liberated. And certainly such desire would be consistent with the divine law. Hence, no man can hold an innocent person to involuntary servitude, without violating the Savior's law of love. For in doing thus he does to another what he would not wish another to do to him.*

But Rankin never sent the letters. Instead, he published them in the local newspaper, the *Castigator*, in 1826. They were later collected and put into a booklet, *Letters on American Slavery*. It was widely circulated in Ohio and Kentucky. Among other points it covered were that the existence of slavery was opposed to the fundamental principle in the Declaration of Independence that "all men are created equal," that prejudice against blacks was based solely on color, that it was wrong to believe people of color didn't have feelings like whites and that slavery was as harmful to the slaveholder as to the slave. In 1832, William Lloyd Garrison serialized them in *The Liberator*. A Quaker press also published them, and that edition was used in 1833 by the American Anti-Slavery Society to publish the first of its eighteen editions of *The Letters*. It gave Rankin a national reputation that made him beloved as an abolitionist and hated as an enemy of the slaveocracy.

Reverend Samuel Crothers.
Courtesy Greenfield Historical Society.

Crothers wrote his series of fifteen letters to the *Cincinnati Journal* in 1831, demonstrating the inequity of slavery and racial prejudice:

> *Our treatment of the Africans is a foul stain on our national character....They are everywhere deprived of the privilege of the common schools....In some states, Sabbath schools, for the purpose of teaching Africans to read the Bible, are put under the ban of the law. In* [slave states] *they are forbidden to assemble after dark, the only season on which their masters afford them leisure...if caught in an assembly the majority of which are not whites, they are punished....Magistrates, etc., are required to break open doors, if necessary, and inflict the specified number of lashes...*[and] *privately teaching slaves to read is by several States, made penal. The late acts of some Southern States, decide that anyone who will teach a colored person, bond or free, to read, shall be punished by fine, or whipping, or imprisonment.*

The influence of the evangelic messengers of antislavery cannot be underestimated. The jerks of passion that enthralled their parents spawned a similar reaction for a different, more compelling cause. These convulsions mingled fortuitously with the meeting of Theodore Weld and the aforementioned Charles Grandison Finney in upstate New York in 1825, the latter of whom wrote:

> *Now, the great business of the Church is to reform the world, to put away every kind of sin. The Church of Christ was...designed...to lift up her voice and put forth her energies against iniquity in high and low places—to reform individuals, communities and governments, and never rest until... until every form of iniquity be driven from the earth.*[98]

People could not resist Finney or his message. Six-foot-two with long arms that whirled about when he was preaching, hypnotic eyes that seemed to stare into the eyes of his audience and a dramatic voice that sometimes slipped into mad groaning, Finney made his listeners cry, laugh and writhe in the "jerks" until they fainted. He crushed his listeners with the threat of damnation lest they repent and ask Christ's forgiveness.[99]

By contrast, Weld was unkempt and sometimes couldn't remember people's names or faces or even the day of the week, so preoccupied was he with his thoughts. But once he gave power to them in speech, he transformed. Before he was out of his teens, he discovered this during a three-year, self-initiated lecture tour through which he was able to support himself. Upon returning home, he moved with his parents to Hamilton, New York, where he met Finney, whom he at first rejected before becoming his devoted disciple.[100] Their meeting seems fateful in retrospect.

Several years later, both came under the sponsorship of the wealthy abolitionists Arthur and Lewis Tappan, whose influence and funding fueled abolitionists throughout the antebellum period. Weld landed at Lane Seminary and led the student rebellion in 1834, energizing antislavery not only in southern Ohio but also throughout the nation; Finney became head of theology and later president of the interracial Oberlin College, one of the strongholds of the UGRR, in addition to writing and preaching.[101] Through them, eastern and western abolitionist evangelism joined forces.

While the battle to end slavery had some of its earliest skirmishes in south-central Ohio, it needed a catalyst to set them on fire. This came from the launching of William Lloyd Garrison's weekly newspaper, *The Liberator*. Often, the enemies of the abolitionists were not only slaveholders but also everyday citizens in the North who considered them fanatics and troublemakers. Garrison himself was led through the streets of Boston with a noose around his neck before the city's mayor intervened.[102] Nevertheless, support for immediate emancipation slowly and gradually increased nationwide, and Garrison's unceasing determination gave local abolitionists a newfound inspiration. As Isaac Beck of Sardinia in northern Brown County wrote:

> *When Garrison started his "Liberator" advocating immediate emancipation, they all joined in with increased seal and every Presbyterian Church became a centre of Abolitionism increased by the intelligent and pious of the churches and non-church members. Here was where the U.G.R.R. workers originated. Previously to that occasionally a slave would come across the river on his way to Canada, but no person felt much interest....If he was hungry they would feed him, if he inquired they would tell him the road.*[103]

In 1835, a meeting to form a state antislavery society in Ohio was scheduled for April 22, 1835. The month before, Weld had gone to speak at the intended site to draw local interest. Originally, he had been scheduled in Zanesville, but no one there would allow it. This is hardly surprising when one considers the history of Zanesville, whose settlers were from Virginia and Kentucky. They had been feuding with those in Putnam across the river, who were from New England, since the communities were founded. An incident involving a fugitive from slavery in 1814 aggravated the tensions, which dissipated in the 1820s when both communities joined in their support for Colonization.[104] However, as the antislavery movement exposed the true motives of Colonization, most abolitionists opposed it. The bitter feud between the communities resurfaced.

So, he went across the river to Putnam, where an antislavery society had been formed two years earlier. Even so, his first lecture was greeted by a mob. Weld said of the attack that "a mob from Zanesville came, broke the windows, tore off the gate, and attacked me when I came out with stones and clubs." This did not deter Weld, who continued to give lectures in private homes in Putnam. Finally, he was able to speak in Zanesville. "On the sixteenth night," he said, "hundreds pledged themselves for immediatism. The way for the state convention was prepared."[105] The convention was held on schedule, but after his first meeting in Putnam, a black man was assaulted. The local black community decided to avoid the convention.[106]

According to official accounts, 117 representatives of twenty-five counties attended, with four corresponding members.[107] Threats of violence continued, and A.A. Guthrie, one of Putnam's leading abolitionists, was assaulted with bricks and mud by a mob one evening.[108] One-sixth of the attendees were native southerners, as were three of the four corresponding members—two Lane Rebels and James G. Birney.[109] The guest of honor, Birney, had not yet moved to Cincinnati to publish his antislavery newspaper, *The Philanthropist*.[110]

Other notable abolitionists included Rankin and John B. Mahan, who was quite active in the UGRR with Rankin and Gilliland. The Lane Rebels also were well represented, including Weld and others who would later forge careers as prominent abolitionists: Liberty singer George Clark; fugitive slave missionary Hiram Wilson; and prolific antislavery lecturer Henry B. Stanton, future husband of Elizabeth Cady Stanton.

One of the convention's focal points was a discussion of free blacks in Ohio. The irony of it was the lack of black attendance. The report was prepared by Augustus Wattles, a Lane Rebel, then directing a school for

Above: Stone Academy, Putnam, Ohio. *Courtesy Tom Calarco.*

Right: James Birney. *Library of Congress.*

black children in Cincinnati. Nearly half of Cincinnati's blacks, 1,129, had been slaves, he reported, and many were working to pay off the freedom of family members.[111]

Birney discussed establishing an abolitionist newspaper in Kentucky, which never materialized, and offered a resolution to denounce the Black Laws, calling them "cruel, impious, and disgraceful to a state."[112]

The following year, Weld went to New York and took the job of training abolitionist lecturers for Garrison's American Anti-Slavery Society. He became the leader of the band of seventy abolitionist circuit riders whom Reverend Lyman Beecher, father of Harriet Beecher Stowe, himself a noted evangelist, described as "he-goat men…butting everything in the line of their march" and "made up of vinegar, aqua fortis, and oil of vitriol, with brimstone, saltpeter and charcoal to explode and scatter the corrosive matter."[113]

From 1836 to 1839, they undertook a holy crusade to abolitionize the North, and by the end of the decade, there were about two thousand antislavery societies with upward of 100,000 members.[114] It wasn't easy, and it took great courage, as facing violent opposition was a common occurrence. Henry B. Stanton wrote that during the period from 1834 to 1846, he was mobbed at least two hundred times.[115] In another incident, the building where an abolitionist was lecturing was fired on with a cannon.[116] Even the highly respected Rankin, one of the "Weld's Seventy," was often confronted by fellow northerners. But they soldiered on, ablaze with their gospel like the old revivalists, seeking salvation by vanquishing the evil of slavery. They followed the mantra of Garrison, who had proclaimed, "I am in earnest—I will not equivocate—I will not excuse—I will not retreat a single inch—AND I WILL BE HEARD."[117]

The battle had just begun, however, and the front line was the farm country of south-central Ohio.

Chapter 6

THE GOD-FEARING PIONEERS

I t was a time when most of the men were sodbusters,[118] as they were called in the legendary tales of the Old West, when all the women were addressed politely as "Ma'am" and the family's prized possession was their horse. The men were boys until the gray in their hair and whiskers became most evident. It was a time when a family could live off the land and mom's homemade was all you could eat, a simpler time when the Lord was uppermost in everyone's mind. But there was evil in the world just like today, and in south-central Ohio in the years before the Civil War, that greatest of all evils was slavery—yet there were those who succumbed to it because of the lure of filthy lucre:

> *There were men in every community without reference to creed or political affiliation, who for the sake of rewards, would at the risk of life, pursue the fugitives to captivity for the hope of gain....On the other hand, there were individuals in every community who from "broadness of mind and bigness of heart" would render assistance to the fleeing slave and help him to a place of security from cruel pursuers.*[119]

It was this dichotomy that made the UGRR so exciting and so dangerous; it was a tension that played throughout Ohio and in many places in the North close to the Mason-Dixon line. Such assistance wasn't available in every Ohio community, however. Across the river into Adams County, some slaveholders had moved there, bringing their slaves, freeing them and using them as servants. Furnace entrepreneur John Means "employed Negro servants" as late as 1835.[120] But according to law, no form of slavery was ever supposed to be allowed in the Northwest Territory, of which Ohio was a part. So it's not surprising that a good number of slave catchers lived there:

> *There resided in that vicinity at the time, recalls a county history, a man named Lindsey and another by the name of Ambus who with their families had recently come into the neighborhood from some place in Kentucky. Lindsey and Amboss had caught a runaway slave and returned him to his master across the Ohio, and received for their services the sum of fifty dollars each.*[121]

Another account comes from the grandson of an Adams County slave catcher:[122]

> *The early newspapers, which Adams County people read, contained offers of a reward for return of slaves escaping from the South. Grandfather [Fountain Pemberton] was not averse to such appeals, and when opportunity presented would assist in capturing and returning the slaves and accepted the reward offered.*
>
> *One morning an escaping slave came along and grandfather set him down to breakfast. While the colored man was eating, grandfather secured a rope and was about to secure him, but the man was alert and taking in the situation, he whipped out a razor and made his escape.*
>
> *Many people knew of grandfather's capturing runaways.*

These are only two examples, but the stories of slave catchers in Ohio are in the hundreds. The closer to the border, the more likely they might find some slave catchers going for breakfast at the local tavern on a regular basis. It's probably what was happening in Ripley, where the shootout with the Rankin boys at the Rankin homestead is certainly the stuff of legend. So, while there was still a lesser threat of slave catchers across the county's northern border, they knew no boundaries.

Fugitives made their way north in Adams County through Simon Kent's Trace from the Ohio River, the natural pathway of green fields made by the ancient buffalo herds, through West Union and the home of Chillicothe Presbytery member Dyer Burgess. Up the hills, they came into Sinking Spring, Highland County, where fugitives found trustworthy friends like the Wickerhams:[123]

The Abolitionists usually availed themselves of the assistance of free men of color to win the confidence and secure control of the escaped slave. During my mother's last illness in 1844 our mulatto man Jason brought to my father's house at Sinking Spring a fleeing slave whose pursuers were hot upon his tracks. He was hastily secreted in a hay mow belonging to a neighbor, when his pursuers consisting of his owner and a posse from West Union with William Lee as leader arrived.…This party had sighted the fugitive and felt sure he was with…the Abolitionists of the village, of whom my father was considered a leader.

The fugitives were hiding in a haymow, Wickerham wrote, and the slave catchers trampled and prodded it with pitchforks. Luckily, the slave catchers didn't find them:

The little village was…patrolled by the slave hunting gang for three days when…Colonel Wilson, John Weyer and Geo F. Dunbar proffered their aid…

A plan was speedily arranged and after night fall of the next day two horsemen with a lead horse between them rode in front of Dunbar's house on the main street, whence a color person emerged and mounting the spare horse, went galloping northward. We heard the reports of the picket's [those surveilling the area] *harmless guns and they all rushed to headquarters for further directions. Simultaneously with this diversion the real fugitive (the other was John Weyer in disguise) dressed in my mother's gown and bonnet was taken out of town by a back street…and proceeded in safety until he reached the settlement of Friends.*[124]

John McElroy—who was born near Greenfield, Highland County, and whose father, Ebenezer, and older brother, Thomas, were UGRR agents—vividly recalled what it was like when a fugitive arrived:

The "coming" of the fugitives was something exciting at our house. We would be waked in the night by the barking of dogs. Then probably a window sash at the rear of the house would be heard "rattling" by the striking with the "edge" of the hand against the bottom rail. To the inquiry "Who's there?" the answer would be "Friends." Then the door would open and in would come Carey Wilson [Adam Wilson] *or Irwin Brooks of Thomas Rodgers* [Rogers], *or Uncle David Thournley* [Ghormley], *with from one to six fugitives. A lunch would be set and heartily eaten. The conductors would say goodbye, the passengers would be disposed of for the night in a spare bedroom, in the garret, or possibly in the barn, and then we would sleep until morning.*[125]

This is an incredibly informative paragraph. Not only does it bring you into the moment when the fugitives arrive, but it also identifies verifiable people, three of whom were leaders of the Paint Valley Anti-Slavery Society. Comprising residents from Highland, Fayette and Ross Counties, it boasted the largest membership of any antislavery society in the state, accounting for 942 members in 1837.

Carey (or Adam) Wilson, who would have been about fifty at the time, was secretary of the Paint Valley society and member of the Greenfield's First Presbyterian Church, whose pastor was Reverend Samuel Crothers. Wilson was short but sturdy and energetic. He kept fugitives in the attic and the barn hayloft and, during the day, in the shadows of his cornfields. He forwarded them in an oxcart that carried fugitives underneath a load of hay.

Thomas Rogers, likely Thomas D. Rogers, who would have been in his early to mid-twenties, was the son of Colonel Thomas Rogers, the first president of the Paint Valley society, and a representative at the state antislavery meeting. The colonel had a reputation as a storyteller and liked to tell about the time he met Daniel Boone, who was a friend of his father's, and his experience serving in the War of 1812. At the organizational meeting in Putnam, the colonel was on the committee responsible for petitions to Congress. However, as students of antislavery know, a gag rule on petitions to Congress regarding slavery was put into effect in 1836 that lasted until 1844. This meant that no discussion of slavery was permitted in Congress, suspending the fundamental right of the Constitution to petition Congress. It was a reflection of the power the South had to impose its desire for slavery, something that eventually resulted in the Civil War.

"Uncle David" was David Ghormley, the brother of John's mother. He was then about Adam Wilson's age. A delegate at the state society convention in 1839, his son, Hugh, was on the Paint Valley society's executive committee and a state society convention delegate. His brother, William, an elder of the Greenfield Presbyterian Church, also aided fugitives. David's daughter, Elizabeth, was another Ghormley member of the antislavery society. Last but not least, Reverend William Dickey, longtime pastor of the Bloomingburg Presbyterian Church, just up the road in Fayette County, married a Ghormley.

McElroy House. *Courtesy Greenfield Historical Society.*

Wilson House. *Courtesy Greenfield Historical Society.*

Ghormley House. *Courtesy Greenfield Historical Society.*

The Paint Valley Anti-Slavery Society became so large that it split into several smaller societies at some point that included the town of Greenfield and Fayette and Ross Counties. If there is a truism in the study of the UGRR, it's that almost all antislavery society members were potential UGRR agents. So, with nearly one thousand members in a three-county area whose total population was about sixty thousand,[126] it could be said that help for the fleeing fugitive was likely close within reach. This is not surprising when one considers the powerful influence of the Chillicothe Presbytery whose pastors—Samuel Crothers, William Dickey, James Dickey and Hugh Fullerton—served the Presbyterian churches of Greenfield, Highland County; Bloomingburg, Fayette County; and South Salem, Ross County, for combined total of 128 years.[127]

Reverend Fullerton, whose mentor was Reverend Crothers, described a harrowing experience during his early years as pastor of a church in Chillicothe. After an antislavery meeting, Fullerton was confronted by a mob. They began shouting at him. "They want to see a Presbyterian preacher run," he later said, "but I could not give them that happiness." Instead, he kept his composure. "If they could have succeeded in starting me, I believe they would have killed me."[128]

Chillicothe was a town settled by southerners of wealth who brought their slaves and freed them and then continued using them as servants. Fullerton urged the education of these untutored former slaves and brought in a teacher. But the congregants refused to accept her and derided her with the epithet "nigger school mistress."[129] This hostility to antislavery in Chillicothe was not limited to Fullerton. John Rankin also was mobbed when he gave two lectures there in 1835.[130] According to Joseph Skillgess, an UGRR worker who lived ten miles west of the city, its UGRR operation was confined to a small group of black men that included Charles Langston during his residence there. Most UGRR activity was in Ross County's western region.[131] Dr. G.A. Harmon, whose father was active in Frankfort, Ross County, said that mobs "stoned" Robert Stewart and James Jackson, who lived in Ross County, because of their abolitionist views.[132] So, it is not surprising that after four years as pastor of the church in Chillicothe, Fullerton resigned.

Reverend William Dickey. *Courtesy Greenfield Historical Society.*

Nevertheless, the Chillicothe Presbytery continued its strong stand in favor of immediate emancipation, which was unabated until the end of the Civil War. In 1835, the synod issued a number of resolutions. Among them were the following:

> *Resolved, That to offer a slave his freedom only on condition that he will leave his country and go into a foreign land, is unjust and cruel, and ought to subject a church member to censure.*[133]
>
> *Resolved, That when a master advertises a reward for a runaway slave, against whom no other crime is alleged than escaping from his master, he is guilty of a scandalous sin…*
>
> *Resolved, That to apprehend a slave who is endeavoring to escape from slavery, with a view to restore him to his master, is a direct violation of divine law…*[134]

Smith House. *Courtesy Greenfield Historical Society.*

Religion was not the only bond that strengthened the antislavery movement in the region. As in the example of the Ghormleys and the McElroys, family ties were common not only in the Highland/Fayette County area but also in many UGRR communities in the North.[135]

William Smith, whose grandfather and father were officers of the Paint Valley Anti-Slavery Society, wrote down a revealing recollection. He identified Thomas McElroy and William Templeton as his associates and said that they transported fugitives to the home of William Ghormley and, in one instance, escorted ten individuals, most of them children (one of whom later died in Oberlin). Ghormley sometimes accompanied them to a Mr. Hopkins in Washington Court House, who in turn took them to Bloomingburg. He described the roads as "very bad" and said that most often the fugitives had to be moved on horseback. As in most cases described in Ohio's UGRR, movement was done at night and by young men in their late teens or early twenties, with their fathers and other relatives or friends coordinating their movements. You can almost see the stars and hear the hoots of the owls. One time a "stout" black fugitive came and asked for work:

[He] fell in love with a comely yellow girl in the neighborhood and married her…but the agitation…in the fifties made him fearful of being taken back to slavery. They went to Michigan close to the line where he died. He would tell of his escape from a brutal master, of the blood-hound that had almost caught him, and he killed with a heavy stick, swimming a river.[136]

A most interesting corroboration of events is the telling of the story of Peter Dent, who stayed with the McElroys for a month. Dent, who was a free man, had arranged the escape of seven or more slaves owned by Schultz and Bradley of Washington, Kentucky, during the winter of 1843 or 1844. A reward of $2,200 was offered for them, and an intensive search was made throughout Ripley and the surrounding area, where it was believed they were being hidden. So tight was the surveillance that it was impossible for anyone to go beyond Red Oak without scrutiny. John Rankin's son, R.C., had been chosen to be one of their conductors:

We were compelled to run them from William Minnow's to Aunt Mary Pogue's. When the pursuers came to Pogue's, we would run them to Washington Campbell's, from there to James McCoy's, and from James's to William McCoy's, thence to Kirby Bill Baird's, and thence back to Aunt Mary Pogue's, thence to Minnow's and across the woods to Campbell's, and so on.[137]

After several days, James Henry, who was well known and trusted, came to where Rankin was hiding with them. He said he had been feeding the slave hunters and suggested that R.C. bring them to his place and hide there. He reasoned that the slave hunters would never suspect him, not only because he was feeding them but also because his place was so remote it would have been unlikely that fugitives would find it. The fugitives were hidden upstairs, and R.C. actually had dinner with the slave hunters. The next morning, a group of armed men came to escort Rankin and the fugitives to William and Patsy McIntire's place in North Liberty, a village in western Adams County. From there they were taken to Greenfield. McElroy described it:

[Dent's] wife [Fanny] and three children, his wife's sister, and her husband, and one other colored man, had escaped together….They were hotly pursued and to diminish risk they had been separated, scattered among "friends" in different places and some of them kept hidden for days and weeks in the same place. Dent was a free Negro, very black, blind of an eye

and a devout Methodist. He had with him a large pistol, a bowie-knife, and a rifle. His wife and children and the wife's sister arrived a few nights later. The wife…was actually a white woman, with long brown hair, just a little wavy.…Their story was that the master was a kind, good man but that he had become insolvent, his property likely to be sold for debt, with the prospect that the slaves would be taken to the New Orleans market[138].… These six were at my father's about a month. It was considered more safe for them to delay there than to push on North and be detained near Lake Erie until the opening of navigation.[139]

Then news came that the slave hunters had stopped at the hotel in Greenfield. They had a proclamation from Ohio governor Wilson Shannon that had been produced at the demand of the governor of Kentucky. It offered a reward of $500 for the apprehension of Dent, "who had stolen his own wife, and children and three other slaves."

That day at our house was a very anxious one. The fugitives were hid away in various places, some of them concealed in the hay mow. Friendly men, muscular and courageous, dropped in one by one to visit us. At dark two curtained carriages were in readiness. The passengers were stowed away in them, and with two brave men to watch each conveyance, as driver and guard they struck out. They went South then East, then South again, passing within sight of the "hunters".…and onto Twin Hills, ten miles from our house.[140]

Suffice it to say, they arrived safely in Canada. But the story doesn't end there. McElroy, who attended Jefferson College in Pennsylvania from 1849 to 1855 to study for the ministry, eventually becoming licensed by the Chillicothe Presbytery, was passing through Buffalo, New York, in 1853. The word had been passed that Peter Dent had changed his name to George Howard and had moved them. Looking them up in the city directory, McElroy decided to visit:

[I] found my way to the neat, cozy frame dwelling.…Responding to my knock, Fanny made her appearance. She was evidently troubled at sight of this stranger and fearful of his errand.[141] When I ask if this was where George Howard lived, with hesitation and trembling, she said yes. I hastened to relieve her anxiety.…Great relief and joy came to her with the knowledge that I was one of the McElroy family, who had befriended her

and hers when liberty and even life was at stake.... "George" was at work
at the foundry and "Mose" her boy was working on a boat.[142]

Another fascinating story is the legend of Augustus West. A free black man, he migrated with his wife, Harriet, from Madison County, Virginia, to the Greenfield area in 1837, where they eventually had eleven children. He was working near the McElroy farm and apparently hung out at the local general store, which was a meeting place for black and white folks. According to the legend, West proposed a hornswoggle[143] to Alexander Beatty, suggesting that they travel into the South and that Beatty claim West was his slave and sell him. Then Beatty would help him escape, and they would split the profits. They did this three times. On one occasion, West was sold for $1,700 (upward of $35,000 today). At this time, however, no other details about where or how the transactions took place are known.

With the money, West purchased a 55-acre plot of land. He lived on it for fifteen years, during which he cleared it and divided it into two plots. With the money he received from the sale of the land, he was able to purchase a much larger plot of land, 177 acres in all. Here West built his "mansion." It is said that West designed his mansion so that it would be useful as a UGRR stop, although this would have been in about 1858, shortly before the Civil War. On the second floor, it contained a hidden room for which there was no door—it could only be accessed by a ladder from the outside. In addition, he also built a number of cabins on the land that, some believe, were to be used as homes for fugitives from slavery. A dead-end road, which West called "Abolition Lane," provided access to the settlement, which was not visible from the main road. This was done intentionally to protect those who settled there. People did live there during West's life, according to old records, but their identities are not known. In 1883, West sold the property. Today, nothing remains of his house or the cabins, and it is not known when or where he died. His life is in many respect is still a mystery.[144]

There were a fair number of Stewarts in all three counties who were members of the Presbyterian Church, so as might be expected, they became part of the UGRR. Most prominent were the Stewart brothers Robert and James. They were originally from Maryland and came to Ross County with their family when it was still a wilderness. James moved to Bloomingburg and fought in the War of 1812. When he returned, he was appointed to be a colonel in the Fayette County militia. He was one of the early sponsors of the abolitionist Bloomburg Presbyterian Church, the future church of Reverend Dickey, and services were often held in his barn. He also was the

Augustus West's "mansion."

community's most respected citizen, as R.S. Dills's *History of Fayette County* concludes, "He was not surpassed in the community, in his administrative abilities, his Christian character, energy, and liberality."[145] A devoted abolitionist, he was the chairman pro tem of the organizational meeting of the state society in Putnam.[146]

Brother Robert lived in nearby Frankfort, where the family originally settled. He became very active in the UGRR, as testified by his son, J.P.:

> *Bloomingburg was a great abolition hole, after a few years they found a shorter route and went west of* [Frankfort] *on what was known as the Rocky Spring and Greenfield route, thence to Bloomingburg....We kept the slave through the day (secreted). Took them at night on horse or in wagon....There was no special system of communication. We were always on the lookout for them and when they came and thumped on my father's window he knew what was up and stowed them away....One time 12 men ran away together from Ky, agreed to go to Canada or die in the attempt. There was a $10,000 reward offered for their capture and return. There were men sent from Ky to hunt* [them]. *They got others to help in the neighborhoods....The day they were looking...the 12 men were stored in a cabin near Bloomingburg, 20 miles from us. They watched our gates all night. Same night Wm A. Ustick and George Gillespie took them in a four-horse wagon toward the North Star...before*

Early Ohio Underground Railroad. *Map of Wilbur Siebert, drawn by J. Richard Lawwill.*

they got to Cleveland, their masters were there....They were taken on the boat without being seen...told the captain their master was there, he told them to lay low...when he steamed up he paraded the slaves on deck and told them to wave their master goodbye.[147]

An interesting point that was repeated by Stewart in his letter was that the route changed and that there wasn't much traffic at his father's stop after 1845. This was a common occurrence along the UGRR. As the nation grew and better roads and modes of transportation were made available, or people moved or died, the route taken would be modified. Sometimes it was just a matter of overuse or because a route was put under surveillance. This may have caused the slowdown in traffic there. This is only speculation, as a multitude of factors could have been responsible.

A sidelight to the Stewart family is the story of a fugitive slave who came with a baby and left it with the family of George Stewart because he had become ill. As the son of the colonel, George raised the boy, who went on to become a surgeon who settled in Lexington, Kentucky. Family and human relations are so much about the UGRR. It's sad that some historians denigrate its memory and disrespect these relations, which were borne of true human emotion rather than greed or self-aggrandizement.

One of the questions asked by Siebert in his "Circular," referenced in chapter 2, was what period had the greatest traffic of fugitives. Answers varied, and for many in Ohio, it was between 1840 and 1850. Some said that they either stopped their involvement or only were occasionally involved after the Fugitive Slave Act of 1850 for fear of prosecution. But that didn't stop others, as we will see. That was fortunate because that was when the traffic actually increased, as did the boldness and the reach of the slave catchers. In actuality, they had already become very brazen by then, as the Kentucky raids of the 1840s into Michigan to apprehend fugitive slaves illustrate.[148]

To give you an idea what the people in Highland and Fayette Counties thought of the fugitive slave law, these resolutions were passed by the Chillicothe Presbytery in 1851:

Resolved. That no intelligent and conscientious man ought to feel himself bound to regard the requirements of the fugitive slave law…

Resolved. That to assist slave-hunters to catch men, women, and little children who are escaping from slavery, or in any way to assist in carrying out a law so flagrantly unrighteous as the fugitive slave law is a sin…

Resolved. That the authority and laws of the Most High God are paramount; and therefore when the laws of man's making contravene His authority and laws, by making a penal offence to discharge any of the duties we owe to God or our fellow man—such as feeding the hungry, clothing the naked, or receiving the stranger, knowing him to be claimed—or by requiring us to assist the oppressor in catching human beings who are escaping from a land where they are held as chattels, deprived of their inalienable rights and the means of salvation—we should obey God rather than men.[149]

Chapter 7

FRIENDS AGAINST SLAVERY

I n Larry Gara's *Liberty Line*, published in 1961, he set out to correct what he believed were the misconceptions of the UGRR canon. One was that all Quakers were involved in the UGRR.[150] But he took it another step by claiming that the only Quakers involved were a small, radical minority. It is true that some of the most prominent UGRR conductors were Quakers and that they were disowned for their extroverted abolitionism: Levi Coffin, Isaac T. Hopper and Laura Haviland. However, disassociation as a result of conflicts over slavery occurred in every major religious sect.[151] Quakers were little different despite their historical opposition to the peculiar institution.

When one looks at the total picture of the UGRR, especially in Ohio, one comes to a different conclusion about their involvement. For instance, two of the state's most active UGRR centers were Quaker communities: Mont Pleasant and Alum Creek. The Quaker community of Salem also was very active and the home of the *Anti-Slavery Bugle*, the state's longest-running and most important antislavery newspaper, whose founder, Abby Kelley Foster, was a Quaker who was also disowned. Numerous other smaller Quaker communities that had involvement are identified in the Siebert Collection, including Harveysburg and Springboro in Warren County, the town of Chester in Clinton County, and the Green Plain Meeting in Selma, Clark County. Continuously, respondents to Siebert mention Quaker communities in Ohio that were places of refuge. As one wrote, "In fact, it may be said truthfully that wherever there was a Quaker settlement or family that was a 'station'…and help for the runaway slave."[152] She was so right, as any

Quaker who supported slavery was disowned. The disagreements arose over the public expressions and means used to oppose it.

But Gara's observation is partially accurate and helps us to focus better on the reality that was the UGRR, not the myths that have grown. Despite this, myths become popular because they capture our imagination; for instance, the quilt fable has become perhaps the most popular fabric of the UGRR legend. At the same time, we must not forget that the UGRR did exist; that people stayed up all night taxiing fugitives away from the horrors of slavery and did it for only the goodwill that it would bring; that some worked day and night to make money to support this business of helping people to freedom, like Levi Coffin and Thomas Garrett, both of course who were Quakers; and that thousands of people in the North had some involvement, from all religious denominations, even if it were just supplying horses or articles of clothing.[153] Yes, they were breaking the law, but they were following the higher law.

Along the banks of the Little Miami River, in the hilly countryside north of Cincinnati, stands an old stone house, a relic of slower days, when there was lots of land and few people. It is not lived in much these days, but a big family of Quakers lived there for many years. Their forefather, Benjamin Butterworth, was a six-foot, six-inch pioneer, a giant of a man who was said to have weighed three hundred pounds. His roots in America dated back before the 1700s. Born in Virginia, Butterworth was able to purchase the rights to the land in Loveland through the Sackville King Survey of the land in the Virginia Military District, which contained much of the future state of Ohio. This land and his inheritance provided him with substantial wealth. He was like many future Ohioans who would settle the new state: a slaveholder who freed his slaves and took them along to where there was no slavery.[154] While all Quakers in America were forbidden from owning slaves, lest they face disownment, by the time of the Revolutionary War, Benjamin was not a Quaker and only converted later, perhaps at the time of this move.

On September 15, 1812, he set out with his family and some former slaves in two covered wagons to cross the old green Appalachian mountains of what is now West Virginia. It was a trek of more than three hundred miles up mountains more than four thousand feet high through scenic passageways like those that had inspired trailblazers like Daniel Boone a generation earlier. There was only one road through this wilderness, the Midland Trail, which ran along the Kanawha River and today is Route 60.[155] Benjamin, forty-six; his wife Rachel, forty-seven; Moorman, nineteen; Benjamin Jr., eighteen; Samuel, fourteen; Rachel, twelve; William, ten; and

Butterworth House. *Courtesy Tom Calarco.*

Henry Thomas (called by his middle name), three, made the journey in twenty-five days. One can only imagine the sunsets blazing their fire in that pristine wilderness of future promises. In the years ahead, their lives would soon be afire with the cause of abolition.

When Butterworth arrived, he found that his 1,500-acre property needed a lot of work to make it suitable for farming. Although it had the advantage of natural springs and the Little Miami River, it needed clearing and was hilly and full of gullies. It would take time to make it livable. Instead, he took the family to nearby Waynesville, where one of his older daughters, Polly, already was living with her husband, Zachariah Johnson. Within a week, Benjamin purchased land along nearby Caesar's Creek, where they moved. Busy with his farming and building a mill, he ignored his other property for the next three years.

In 1815, Moorman visited it and found a squatter who had built a cabin and planted crops on five acres he had cleared. He bought the cabin and the crops and moved in. Three months later, his older sister Milly and her husband, John Dyer, migrated from Virginia and moved in with him. They built a two-story log cabin, and one year later, Benjamin and the family joined them. By 1820, the old stone house overlooked the fields, as it does today along the Little Miami Bike Trail. In future years, the Butterworth

71

farm grew prosperous through the sale of sweet potatoes and chickens and their eggs, as well as through the construction of the Little Miami Railroad, which ran through their property, connecting south to Cincinnati by 1843 and north to Springfield by 1846.

For a time, a least up until 1850 and the passage of the stronger Fugitive Slave Act, their most important business was the UGRR. Being Quakers, they were stirred by the movement for immediate emancipation of the slaves that already had many supporters in this section of Ohio. Slaves had begun running away more than ever as more in the North joined the effort to assist them. The Little Miami River was a natural gateway. When they exactly became involved in aiding them is not known, but it was probably no later than 1830–31, when their sons William and Thomas married into the Wales and Linton families, Quaker abolitionists who may already have been part of the UGRR.

Thomas's wife, Nancy, was a Wales, and her sister Jane married Valentine Nicholson. It was a double wedding. William married Elizabeth Linton. So, it became an all-in-the-family UGRR operation. Thomas recalled those days shortly before his death in a letter to Wilbur Siebert:

> We [once] *had two women, one man and some children on hand and had them concealed for some time and it was becoming unsafe to keep them longer.…I had two good horses and a good wagon with high sides and a good set of bows and cloth. I put the bows on and then stretched the cloth on and tied it thoroughly down.…After thus being all fixed I stored in a lot of hay for the poor creatures to lie on. Then after leaving all the children* [the fugitives' children] *for fear of their crying and betraying us, I put in two carts for my daughter Mary and I to sit on. By this time we had heard that a pro-slavery boy by the name of Andrew Davis had somehow got a knowledge of the whole thing and had, perhaps for a sum of money, made it known to two persons who would do anything they could to catch the flying slaves. The names of these two persons* [were] *David Coddington and James Foster. We had heard of our betrayal; I prepared for it; the river was high. My destination was to take them to an uncle of my wife's by the name of Turner Welch residing at Harveysburg.…The bridge here at Foster's must be crossed and was a toll bridge. Joseph Whitney took the toll at the west and James Foster kept a store at the east end* [just before they came to the bridge]. *We had our Quaker school teacher, Robert Way, to go with us to see if we should run the gauntlet…just as we expected out came the two men* [Coddington and Foster].[156]

Foster called out to him, "Got any chickens, got any eggs, got any butter."

Butterworth shouted back as he passed by, "I am not going to market I am after fruit trees," and handed Whitney the toll with stopping.

He heard Coddington say to Foster, "I'll be damned if there ain't niggers in that wagon." Butterworth had thought they would follow him and kept looking back, but they made it safely to his wife's uncle on the north side of Caesar's Creek. He did not consider it safe to keep them that night, so he sent them over to Harveysburg up on one of the many hills in that area, and Butterworth returned home to see about the fugitives' children. He gave the task to his neighbor, a man by the name of Carroll, who lived only a mile away and with whom he had a regular arrangement regarding the transport of fugitives:

> *I had a small one or two-horse wagon. I had a neighbor a mile from me who was as strong an anti-slavery man as myself. As far as worldly goods were concerned he had nothing, was rich enough to have a wife and children to help him be poor. He feared no risks in helping fugitive slaves....I told him that when fugitives were on hand that he knew of, to come and get this wagon and one or two horses, as the case would require, and take them, and I would have no questions, and he should ask me none and go in the night, and go to such underground station as we know best, which was at or near Harveysburg...This man Carroll took those children up there where they no doubt found their mothers.*[157]

One of the Carroll family members recalled the nights he spent transporting fugitives for the Butterworths:

> *Often, in this wild flight for freedom, the master, with his unhuman helpers was in close pursuit, armed...devoid of mercy, protected by the law, and supported by a public sentiment that was respectable...Whether the pursuit was or was not immediate and pressing, it was always probable and expected, so that the runaway was in the condition of the hunted...*
>
> *The people that helped [fugitives]...had no rational hope of compensation. On the contrary, they gave aid, with the certainly of the loss of time and money, and with the possibility of fines and imprisonment.*
>
> *One early morning I was told to go up in the haymow. On doing so I was somewhat startled to see half a dozen black persons hidden away. That day they lay hid and their food was carried to them with secrecy. About 9 o'clock that evening we hitched up, [and] cautiously loaded the*

vehicle with its human freight, and carefully fastened down the curtains. Thomas Butterworth was there and assisted. It was raining; the sky was still clouded and the roads wet and muddy. We went at first by a lane, across the farm of Butterworth, another of the brothers....We soon struck the main road and turned our course towards the North Star....We drove along at a round pace, always on the lookout for pursuers, and it must be confessed, somewhat nervous. Now and then we stopped, and by the struggling moonbeam's misty light, carefully scanned the road in both directions. We crossed Todd's Fork near the site of Morrow; drove past Rochester and Clarksville and on through the night to Harveysburg, where we arrived just after daylight. As we traveled along the stories of the blacks were told.[158]

In one, a slave trader had come to their plantation, which meant the possibility of being sold to the Deep South, where they would be overworked in brutal conditions with the likelihood of dying an early death. Another was family of three, whose twelve-year-old daughter was under consideration of being sold away. They stole a skiff and rowed down the Licking River to Cincinnati. A third told of a man who contracted out to work and earn money, which he was using to pay for the freedom of both himself and his wife. Unfortunately, his wife was owned by a different master—a Baptist minister, in fact—who sold her away to the Deep South.

"Scruples of conscience at violating the Fugitive Slave Law readily vanished before such narrative[s]," he said.

Ready to vanquish any such scruples was an eccentric and intensely intellectual abolitionist and freethinker, Orson S. Murray, who moved into the Butterworth neighborhood sometime in the early 1840s. With long hair and a scraggy beard, he was an unappealing, atheistic version of Jesus Christ. He had come from Vermont, where he'd been a fiery antislavery speaker who antagonized the already angry mobs gathering at antislavery lectures all over the North. Here in remote Ohio, he found some solitude, a haven for his ideas and people who would tolerate him.

Murray already had done some writing in metaphysical journals of the day and had published his own newspaper in Vermont, the *Telegraph*. He started another newspaper, the *Regenerator*, not far from the Butterworth backyard. Its motto: "Ignorance was evil and knowledge its remedy."

Here's what William Burleigh, the brother of eccentric antislavery speaker Charles Burleigh, after whom Murray named one of his children, wrote about the *Regenerator*: "Mr. Murray appears to be a benevolent and self-denying man—is very eccentric in his appearance—very wild in many of his notions—and a very unsafe leader, for he leads into the mazes of skepticism and infidelity."[159]

Murray provided his own description of the *Regenerator*: "If the Regenerator has helped to dispel and disperse the delusion, that that book [the Bible] is the voice of a god—and to show that it is only the words of men—men, some of them, in profound ignorance and darkness on the subjects they were pretending to elucidate—it has done something towards accomplishing one of the principal objects which have impelled me to do the very unpopular work of publishing it."[160] Legends say that he might have helped some fugitives too. He lived until 1885, dying at the age of seventy-eight.

Butterworth's daughter Jane also wrote to Siebert of her memories when she was about six or seven years old:

> *Among my earliest recollections, I was awakened about sunrise by the stopping of my father's large wagon and two horse, and* [him] *handing me a little child 5 or 6 years old over to the care of a thrifty woman* [who had come] *out of a well-kept farmhouse, while he gave a shrill whistle for the men to come up from the field. I was taken into the house and seated in a small chair. The woman then gave me some freshly baked ginger bread while father talked with the man. I did not understand so unusual a visit at that place and time of my life for nothing was explained to me and I saw no people of color, heard no words, but I was sure there was such in our wagon. But as I grew older and learned about the Underground R.R, I knew that we were in that business then.* [After] *that time I* [went] *with my father on this said business when I was old enough to know about it. Several times I remember mother coming to our bedroom late at night and getting* [us] *all up in a hurry and putting us in bed elsewhere to give our bed to a lot of fugitives who come weary and tired, and our grandmother* [Rachel, who died in 1848] *would tell them to "go to sleep, you will be safe in that room, nobody will get you there."*[161]

Thomas said his brother William, who lived a few miles north in Maineville, probably helped twice as many as him. How many is not known, although Thomas said he probably helped as many as one hundred. Family anecdotes, however, suggest more, including stories of single parties numbering as many as twenty-six, belying Thomas's count. The important thing, though, was that all were brought safely to freedom. "I can say in truth that such was

Jane Nicholson. *Courtesy Ohio History Center.*

our success that I do not believe a single one was ever re-captured and taken back to slavery," he said.

The Butterworths' involvement in the UGRR was certainly influenced by their sons' marriages with the Wales and Linton families in the Harveysburg area. The Waleses were related to Levi Coffin, and Thomas's brother-in-law, Valentine Nicholson, was among the most radical abolitionists of his day and a freethinker, a little like Murray. He was immersed in the progressive ideas of the time, including women's rights, phrenology, spiritualism and communal living. In addition to farming, he also was a printer and publisher of books that reflected his progressive views. While it is not clear if wife Jane was fully in agreement with all of his passions, one thing both were passionate about was ending slavery. As she recalled from her childhood:

> I was eight years old when my parents settled in their new home but the sad scenes of slavery I witnessed in Carolina are fresh in my mind [she was then seventy-nine]....A neighbor of our who wanted money to travel sold to the trader the only child of a slave woman, a little girl about my age. The mother cried and grieved so she wasted to a shadow....We heard her screams and were so distressed....When I grew older I resolved to do what I could to break up the traffic in flesh and blood.
>
> For 25 years...[the fugitives] stopped at my house, ate at my table. I heard their tales of hardship; their desire for freedom, and the danger and sacrifice they were making to obtain it. They were often scarred with the whip and torn with the teeth of dogs. Many of them had been out for weeks hiding in swamps and thickets by day and traveling by night....Many of the house servants who had been treated kindly were strongly attached to the family of their master, but it was the dread of being sold in the event of their master's death that determined many of them to escape. The waiting maid of the wife of a member of Congress from Little Rock was going to Washington with them but left at Cincinnati. Delicate and out of health she stayed with us for some time before she was able to go on; she had

cared for her mistress from infancy and every morning would say, "my poor mistress, I wonder who is dressing her and combing her pretty hair."

One man came back Canada with a year to get his wife from Kentucky. She was not able to go with him when he ran away for she had a young babe. In a few weeks he came back with his young wife, but they had left their child, six years old. I cried out in astonishment. They said it was impossible to escape with it. At midnight they left it in bed and concealed themselves under the fodder until the search for them was made and abandoned. They heard the hounds baying and the men talking [and] heard them walking on the fodder over them spearing it with pikes and pitchforks, but went away saying they are not here...

In the record of one year the number that came was 86, but in other years, I know we had many more.[162]

Valentine Nicholson also wrote to Siebert. He stated that his first interaction with a fugitive slave "was in the spring of 1831." Interestingly, he refers to himself here in the third person:

The Friends in Cincinnati sent them up Foster's Crossing in the Butterworth neighborhood, sometimes, and to Springboro or Harveysburg, at other times, according to the emergency of the case....In the first mentioned neighborhood one of the trusted friends of the slave was William Butterworth. In the same vicinity was Henry T. Butterworth. At Springboro lived Edward Potts and John Potts, and Warner M. Bateman....[Valentine Nicholson] was generally known to be a reliable and trusted friend of all those escaping from Southern bondage and consequently most of those escaping from Cincinnati...were delivered to his care.

He mentioned some prominent abolitionists who spoke in Harveysburg: Joshua Giddings, Stephen S. Foster (Abby Kelley's husband), Charles Burleigh and Parker Pillsbury; others in nearby Oakland who spoke were Frederick Douglass, Sidney Howard Gay, Charles Redmond and John Wattles, among others. He added that he attended a meeting with John Rankin in Jamestown, Greene County.

Valentine Nicholson. *Courtesy Ohio History Center.*

He recalled Rankin saying, "If you convince me that the Bible supports such an institution I will trample the Bible under my feet."

I generally kept a span of one or two of good work-horses, one farm or market wagon and one light two-horse carriage. Only on one occasion did I ever permit one of these passengers to travel on foot alone…and that was when the young man felt anxious to continue his journey.

At one time, there was a band of colored musicians [eight in number] *on their journey from New Orleans to Canada. They had the finest and most costly finished and ornamented set of musical instruments that I ever saw.…Their master, it seems, was a gentleman of New Orleans, who had selected them on account of their musical tastes and skill, and had procured instruction for them so as to have a complete popular band to play for balls and parties. Their service was in such demand as to appear like the promise of regular and handsome income to the master.…The leader of the band appeared always so trustworthy and prompt in handing over to the master the money they received while they were off on excursions that when they made him what seemed like a generous offer of their time he accepted the proposition. So they had the liberty to go wherever they seemed to be in the most demand for their services, earning plenty of money to enable them to settle promptly for their time. Some captains of steamboats were acquainted with the fact that they went to different cities on the river, paying the master for their time and returning when they chose. So one winter as the time of the holidays drew near they gave master to understand that they were going away as far as Louisville, KY, But when the boat got to Louisville, they neglected to get off until the boat had reached up the river. At Cincinnati they went ashore, and some way got the notion in their heads that if they should go off on a visit to Canada, and after they got there do as they pleased about returning again to their master it would benefit them as much as it would injure their master. I took them 15 miles on their way to Canada to the neighborhood of Green Plain; I left them in the care of Thomas Swain. I afterwards heard of their safe arrival in Canada.*[163]

In 1858, the Nicholsons separated, as Valentine needed to pursue his missions "to bring mankind into associative communities, or bodies that shall have most or all of what they have in common—as a truly good and loving family."[164] Although they seemed to others an ideal couple, their split had probably been long in coming.[165] In 1842, Valentine had founded the Society for Universal Inquiry and Social Reform. Its mission apparently was to form a perfect communal society, a utopia on earth, and the society became involved in seven such enterprises over the years. The first venture took place in 1844, when the Nicholsons invested $4,000 in Prairie Home in Logan County, the first of these utopias. Its founder was radical abolitionist John Wattles, brother of Lane Rebel Augustus Wattles, who founded a school for blacks in Cincinnati and helped settle newly emancipated slaves in Mercer County, Ohio. An itinerant lecturer, John became interested in Nicholson's society. In 1844, Wattles, who had married Clinton County Quaker Esther Whinery, established Prairie Home, but it failed after a few months. Nicholson continued his efforts, however, with Jane's support, according to letters she wrote. Perhaps with the Civil War looming and his inability to create his heaven on earth, he felt he needed the freedom to seek his mission on his own. Their separation lasted some three decades, but they were finally reunited in Indianapolis a decade before their deaths, he in 1904 at age ninety-four and she in 1906 at age one hundred.[166]

An interesting and little-known story about them is that a highly publicized fugitive had a lengthy stay at their house. Both Jane and Elizabeth told the story to Siebert, and there are other, more detailed accounts about Louis, including one by Levi Coffin, leaving out the last detail, however, of where he sent the fugitive. As Coffin tells the story, Louis had escaped from Kentucky, and after finding work in Cincinnati, he eventually moved to Columbus, where he had lived for several years. Somehow, his master learned of his whereabouts and had a warrant issued for his arrest. Louis telegraphed Cincinnati attorney John Joliffe, who informed Coffin, and they agreed they needed to get a writ of habeas corpus to have Louis released and charge his master with kidnapping. Their defense was that Louis's master had brought him into Ohio while on business at his own volition, which according to Ohio law made him free. The sheriff took the slaveholder in custody when they arrived on the train in Cincinnati. A trial of several days followed, and the judge allowed the slaveholder to return home and get legal representation to prepare his case. Once the proceedings were concluded, the judge declared a recess to the following day to give him time to come to his decision.

On that day, in October 1853, Louis was sitting between the U.S. marshal and his master. The courtroom was packed, and the anticipation flowed down the courthouse stairs and out into the streets. Prefacing his decision, the judge read a long, drawn-out, tedious explanation on the points of law he had to consider. It was enough to put one to sleep, and maybe it did, because gradually Louis was sliding his chair back; those behind him, all abolitionists, were giving him ground:[167]

I was standing close behind him and saw every movement, wrote Coffin. Next he rose quietly to his feet and took a step backward. Some abolitionist, friendly to his cause, gave him an encouraging touch on the foot, and he stepped farther back. Then a good hat was placed on his head by some one behind, and he quietly and cautiously made his way around the south end of the room, into the crowd of colored people on the west side, and…toward the door.…our hearts throbbed with…anxiety lest he should be discovered. The door and passage were crowded with Germans, through whom Louis made his way…passing down stairs gained the street. He…made his way quickly, though with not enough haste to attract attention, through an alley, across the canal, through the German settlement, and by an indirect route to Avondale, where he knew the sexton of the colored burying ground.[168]

It's unclear how long it was before they noticed that Louis missing, but by then he had disappeared. During the next few weeks, he stayed first in a building owned by a colored family and then secretly was moved to a church. He spent several weeks holed up in Cincinnati, and then it was decided to create a ruse for him to escape. They sent a telegraph from Columbus that Louis had passed through on a train bound for Cleveland, and it was published in the newspaper. They followed it up with a dispatch that he was on a boat headed for Detroit:

Finally, a Presbyterian minister [Dr. Boynton] *and his wife, who were in Cincinnati for a short time, offered to convey him out of the city. Arrangements were accordingly made, and they drove their buggy to the church door one morning about nine o'clock. Louis, disguised as a woman with a veil over his face, entered the carriage and sat on the back seat by the lady. They took him about thirty miles out of the city to a noted depot of the Underground Railroad.*[169]

As Jane Nicholson tells it, they arrived at the Nicholsons around sunset, and her younger daughters saw him come in. "[They were] rather astonished to see an awkward mulatto woman go upstairs and come down a brisk slender man."[170]

Chapter 8

THE LIBERATORS

In May of 1843 Dr. Edwin Fussell came to an anniversary meeting [of the American Anti-Slavery Society] *in New York with a large company of Ohio abolitionists in a monster wagon built by Abram Allen and called "The Liberator."*[171]

The Liberator was a legend in its day in the south-central region, but it was almost unknown outside the region and eventually became lost to history. Siebert gave it one line and was less descriptive than Smedley. Valentine Nicholson provided what was arguably the best description of it:

> [Abram Allen] *was a very ingenious mechanic. He built himself an omnibus, and it was so often used to help fugitives on the way to Canada, that in speaking of it the neighbors called it "the old Liberator."... Underneath the body of the old Liberator, attached to the axle tree was a clock bell with simple machinery connecting with the hub of one of the hind wheels, so as to cause this clock bell to be struck by a little hammers every time the wheel had rolled over a mile.*[172]

There were other descriptions, and it had many drivers. It symbolized the Harveysburg-Clinton County connection that was probably as well knit as any in the state, certainly in the southern half of Ohio, with the people deserving of the moniker "liberators." Jesse Oren said that his father, Elihu, had as many as six fugitives hidden for days at a time:

Miniature of Abram Allen's "Liberator," which was created by Allen as a gift for Valentine Nicholson. *Courtesy Tom Calarco, Museum of the Friends Home.*

I remember at one time just after he had taken a colored man to the next station while we were eating dinner a man on horseback dashed up to the front of the house and throwing himself from the horse he looked eagerly in at the open door. He claimed to be from Kentucky and looking for a stray horse. My thought at once from the action of the man [was] that he was looking for "niggers." [Elihu] soon learned his suspicions were correct for the man after leaving our house went to a neighbor of ours and stated he was in pursuit of a runaway.[173]

Oren, whose brother married one of the Allen daughters, also had an interesting comment about the Liberator: "I have no idea how many took passage on the Liberator but I know Jacob Allen and I often drove to Paintersville by the light of the stars and deposited our load with good old Joseph Coate, the first station north of our home.

Mark Haynes was a regular driver for the UGRR:

I was the conductor on this railroad and I have gone on many times, but never got caught, but I knew that I was liable to fine and imprisonment but that did not deter me in the least. I went whenever the opportunity

CONDUCTORS IN CLINTON COUNTY, OHIO
Based on the Research of Bernie Quigley
(Clinton County History, Newspapers, Clinton County History Society Files)

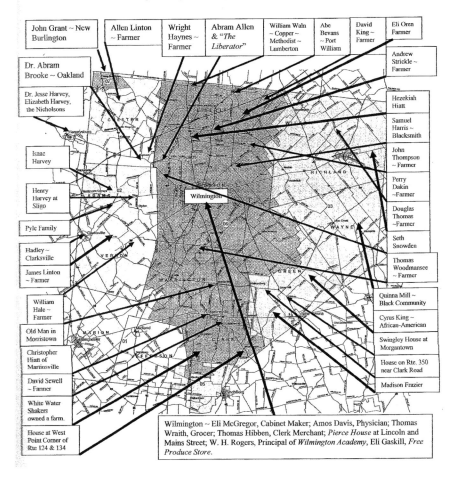

Courtesy Greenfield Historical Society.

offered and it was often that I would start at dusk and travel until I got to the station and it was often daylight before I got there. My route was from Oakland to Xenia, Ohio, and on north as far as Green Plain and our friend Valentine kept a station near Clifton [1839–42], and I almost always gave him a call, and an old Scotchman kept the station at Xenia and he was a genius sure. How well I remember how he talked, although that has been fifty years.

The first time I went to [Allen's] house…Abram told me to tell him I had a load of furniture for him.[174] *I drove up to his house about two in the morning and got the old fellow up and told him I had a load of furniture for him from Abram Allen. He said, "Can it walk?" He knew immediately what I had.*

I remember at one time I had a part of two families, about ten in all, large and small, and I tell you I had a jolly time.[175]

Dr. George M. Dakin married one of Abram Allen's daughters and, in contrast to some accounts, said that there was no abeyance in the UGRR activity after 1850. For those driving the Liberator, it was actually the reverse:

I made my first trip with my father when I was 12 years of age. From that time until I left the state in 1853, I was actively engaged in the work. I became so well acquainted with the road to Port William and Jamestown that I could travel it the darkest nights and signal by a low whistle to the drivers behind although it was rough and there were frequent hills and valleys and bridges and angles. We generally traveled in covered wagons, with a guide on horseback. During the later years several young men of the neighborhood would go on horseback and lead the horses which the fugitives rode the next day.

After the Fugitive Slave Law was passed, the sentiment changed so rapidly, that we often went by daylight. There was a general disposition to defy that effort of the slaveholders, to make every Northern man a bloodhound, but a few timid ones yielded to the fear of arrest. The Anti-Slavery people in that section of the State were many of them Quakers, and we never carried any arms, that is, pistols, revolvers, although there were many times when slave hunters were in the neighborhood, of course.[176]

A picture here is emerging of how the UGRR operated in this part of the country. The hard work of transporting and staying up all night was done by young people, some really still children. One also gets the sense of excitement, of the adventure for these boys. It's a reality that makes sense and lends credence to the stories. It would be much harder for middle-aged men to stay up all night and then go to their jobs during the day. Joel P. Davis got started when he was only fourteen. His father was from Kentucky, but when his life was threatened after refusing to join a slave hunt, he moved to Ohio. "Abram Allen and his son, David…[did] more in this work than anyone else," he said.[177] He used to drive with Mark Haynes and said that

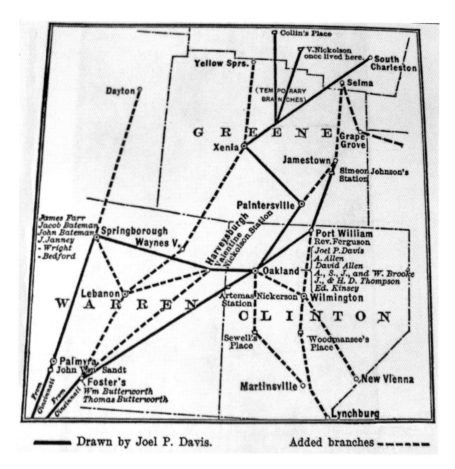

Joel P. Davis map. *From* Slavery to Freedom *by Wilbur Siebert.*

usually two people would convey the fugitives. He became well known among the abolition community through his UGRR work. He said that Warren, Clinton and Clark Counties each had a large number of persons involved. He said it was "hazardous" to go to Dayton.

Davis became an agent for the American Anti-Slavery Society in 1846, entrusted with that duty by fellow agents Valentine Nicholson and Samuel Brooke. This duty involved giving lectures, raising money for the cause and selling subscriptions to the society's three newspapers, *The Liberator*, the *National Anti-Slavery Standard* and the *Anti-Slavery Bugle*. However, he married soon after and moved out of the area, first to Indiana and then to Iowa. He devoted his life to progressive causes, and as he said in his letter to Siebert, he never received any money for his efforts.

Seth Linton lived less than a mile away from the big old "mud house" of Allen. His father was closely involved with Allen, and his sister was the wife of William Butterworth. He said that Allen helped more than three thousand fugitives.[178] He described a trip one day that he and his sister took to Levi Coffin's and also one time when slave hunters came to Allen's place looking for fugitives then being hidden at William Butterworth's; Abram's father played a joke on the slaveholders:

> *I took one in my wagon at Levi's and my sister, Elizabeth Butterworth was with me. We covered the man up in the wagon, left after dark, drove six miles to Sharpsburg on the Montgomery pike to an Englishman's hotel, that was [run by] an anti-slavery man by the name of Holt. The next day got to Wm Butterworth, stayed there all night. The next day to John Hadley's at Clarksville; next day home and left the slave at Abram Allen's. He would send them on to a station.[179]*
>
> *[William] had 12 slaves hid in his place…and when they were at Butterworth's, a company of slave hunters came to Abram Allen's.…There was a cornfield adjoining his weaver's shop and the old Quaker, William Allen run behind the shop and hallooed in a low tone, "Run boys, run boys," and the slave hunters surrounded the corn field.*

Essie Dakin, the daughter of Allen, had some interesting comments about Allen and who he worked with. She said that he often went to Cincinnati and while doing business would pick up fugitives from Levi Coffin, Cornelius Burnett, Henry Lewis or Gamaliel Bailey. She also said the Rankin boys and John Van Zandt would sometimes bring fugitives. She named other cohorts of the local UGRR, including Hezekiah Hiatt near Center, Ohio; Sam Ferguson at Port William; Simeon Johnson at Jamestown; David Monroe in Xenia; and William Thorne and Joseph Dugdale in Green Plain, Clark County, as places her husband took fugitives. She wrote that a $4,000 reward was offered for Allen. According to Thomas Butterworth, Allen wasn't the only one for whom there was a reward for his capture at the time; a $1,000 reward was also offered for his brother, William. Perhaps it was not a coincidence that Thomas also said that William brought more of his passengers to Allen.[180]

According to Beers's 1882 history of the county, the *Clinton County Republican* reported a meeting of the county antislavery society. The president was Wright Haynes and the secretary James Linton, fathers of Mark and Seth; speeches were made by Abram Allen, John Wattles and Abram Brooke. It listed the

UGRR operators as Abram Allen, Aaron Betts, Abel Beven, Abram Brooke, Joseph Coat, Amos Compton, John Grant, Jonathan Hadley, Christopher Hiatt, Thomas Hibben, Allen Linton, Eli McGregor, Elihu Oren, Thomas Wraith, Thomas Woodmansee, John Worth and Doctor Watson.[181]

In Nicholson's account, he identifies most of these men, as well as others. Like Allen, he and Jane must have harbored numbers in the thousands of fugitives. As she said, eighty-six in one year and sometimes more, and they did it for twenty-five to thirty years. Nicholson must have been a special friend of Allen's, or at least Allen had a great deal of respect for his efforts. Perhaps that is why Allen created the miniature of the Liberator as a gift for him.

Amazingly, the miniature replica is currently on display at the Museum at the Friends Home in Waynesville. In 1918, Nicholson's daughter, Mary Ellen, restored the paint, added the inscription "The Steele Bros." and gave it as a gift to her grandsons. The wagon was donated in 1985 by one of the boys to the Mary S. Cook Library, which has it on loan to the museum.[182] What a symbolic relic of those days of UGRR yesteryear.

It should be noted that Abram Allen made a visit to Canada, much like Levi Coffin, to see some of those he helped become free.[183]

If there was a third person to add to a triumvirate of prominent UGRR agitators in the region, it would have to be Dr. Abram Brooke. This is not to say that Valentine wasn't eccentric, but Dr. Brooke was more on the line of John Brown. Tall and thin, Brooke had an unkempt beard and wore plain clothing, a shirt and pantaloons being his normal dress (pantaloons were short pants reaching above the ankle and an unconventional mode of dress). He not only spent time in jail for an incident in Warren County but also a brief time in Canada in 1858, fleeing because rumors had circulated that he was going to be arrested for violating the FSL. Brooke, in fact, likely played a role in the rescue of a slave, just a child, from Salem, Ohio, in 1854.[184]

Brooke did not believe in money. A licensed physician, he gave his medical services free of charge. He explained that once he needed a furnace built to make bricks and that he had any number of locals offer to do it for free. Brooke had lots of interests, including women's rights, for which he was a vocal advocate, as well as many ideas we would call progressive today. But his overriding passion was ending slavery. He had a big barn constructed on his property in Oakland to hold antislavery conventions. It was here where Frederick Douglass spoke in 1843.[185] Imagine thousands coming to hear speakers in such a sparsely populated area.[186] It illustrates the intensity of antislavery feeling in the area. Nicholson described the barn: "[N]eighbors joined together by planting posts in the ground, placing long timbers on the tops of these posts, and covering the structure with clapboards…and provided seats to accommodate thousands. Some called it Liberty Hall, some called it 'the big shed.'"[187]

Brooke had five brothers, and they came from a family of abolitionists, originally from Maryland. The family moved to the Quaker community of Marlboro, Ohio, about ten miles from Salem, in the early 1830s. Brother Samuel, two years younger, was nearly as prominent in the abolitionist movement, becoming the chief agent for the American Anti-Slavery Society in Ohio and its newspaper, the *Anti-Slavery Bugle*. His role was not merely to solicit subscriptions for the *Bugle*, as the case for individual agents listed in the paper, but to promote the antislavery agenda; this is evident when one examines the *Bugle* and finds the number of articles written by Brooke and meetings reporting his involvement. Samuel also found time to write *Slavery and the Slaveholders Religion: As Opposed to Christianity*.[188]

From *Slavery and the Slaveholders' Religion* by Samuel Brooke:

Rev. Joshua Boucher, formerly a minister of the Methodist Episcopal Church, states that the slaves of the South are told that God made them black with the design that they should be slaves; and that, when traveling and preaching in the South, another preacher, belonging to the same church, related the following conversation, which took place between himself and a slave boy:

Minister: "Have you any religion?"
Boy: "No, sir."
Minister: "Don't you want religion?"
Boy: "No, sir."
Minister: "Don't you love God?"
Boy: "What! Me love God, who made me with a black skin and white men to whip!"

In 1839, three of the Brooke brothers—Abram, James and Edward—were involved in an incident that had repercussions for both abolitionists and slaveholders. The following version is based on several accounts.[189]

On November 5, 1839, a slaveholder, Bennett Raines, was passing through the area with his four female slaves—two adults, a mother and daughter, and two grandchildren, one three and the other an infant girl. Word had gotten around during their passage through Clinton County, and

David Monroe House in Xenia. *Courtesy Tom Calarco.*

the abolitionists there sent word ahead. They stopped to rest after passing through Springboro. Meanwhile, a hasty meeting of the town's abolitionists led by Franklin Farr, Mahlon Wright and John Potts was arranged to discuss their options. Attending were the Brooke brothers, who had come from Clinton County with a writ of habeas corpus. It was decided to free the slaves, and they appointed Abram to be the spokesperson and serve the slave owner with the writ if he resisted.

When Brooke informed Raines that his slaves were free under state law, he said that if his slaves wanted their freedom, they could have it. Perhaps to his surprise, the adults were willing and stepped over to the abolitionists with the baby. But the boy was nowhere to found, at first. Apparently, the daughter of Raines had hidden him. After a short search, Brooke pulled a pin out of the ground that supported one of their tents, and he was found. That was when Raines took out his gun, only to hear the sound of revolvers carried by the abolitionists being cocked, causing him to put his gun away. Brooke then served the warrant, and the slaveholder was arrested.

At the court, the judge who issued the writ dismissed the charges, and Raines went to nearby Franklin, Ohio, a proslavery town, and contrived a story that the abolitionists had stolen his money and threatened him with weapons to release the fugitives. But it was too late to get back his slaves, for they had been put on the UGRR with David Allen, who took them to the Green Plain Meeting in the Liberator. It was later reported that they never went to Canada and settled in Ohio.

Seventeen abolitionists were indicted on six charges but were only convicted of intending to make an assault on Raines because they threatened him with weapons to release his slaves—or, as one abolitionist described it, as using force to uphold the law. Brooke said that the only violence that occurred was when he pulled out the pin holding up the tent. Thirteen of the defendants were sentenced to five days in jail and a fine; however, they were released after forty-eight hours when the courts granted a writ of error. Eventually, the case went before the Ohio Supreme Court, which found in favor of the abolitionists in 1841.[190] The case received a great deal of coverage and gave notice to slaveholders to avoid bringing their slaves into the state.

Brooke later wrote about the case in a three-part article[191] after he moved back to Marlboro in November 1853 to become president of the Western Anti-Slavery Society,[192] which had become the state's Garrisonian society attached to the *Bugle*[193] after a fracture of the Ohio Anti-Slavery Society:

> *The mobocrats* [from Franklin] *not satisfied with this, organized a band of forty men to lynch the individual most obnoxious to them, who was accused of stealing the money. As they were 22 miles distant from his residence* [Abram Brooke lived then in Oakland, almost exactly twenty-two miles from Franklin], *their scheme was frustrated by an expression of sentiment by a few, who though not abolitionists were yet unwilling* [that] *the person and property of neighbor should be attacked.*
>
> *The Grand Jury…indicted the accused, for a breach of the laws of Virginia and also of the laws of Missouri, by acts done on Ohio soil!*

Earlier in the article, Brooke discussed a slave rescue in the same vicinity in 1836 in which a local black man rescued ten slaves who were being transported by a slave trader through Ohio and sent them on their way to Canada. In later years, this was one of at least two others that have been conflated with 1839 incident. D. Staley told the story to Wilbur Siebert.[194] It reflected this conflation, putting the date of the incident more than five years after it actually occurred:

> *Some time in the forties there came a slave-holder with* ten slaves *going west, late in the afternoon, camping two miles west of Springboro.…Fred*

Wilson…was working on the road with Mr. Hopkins. Fred being a colored man, the slave owner asked Mr. Hopkins what he would take for that fellow. "He is not for sale," Mr. Hopkins relied. Fred said to Mr. Hopkins, "His'n wont be sale very long." The master had gone to a farmhouse, leaving his slaves in camp, giving Fred a good chance to operate that night, which he was not slow in doing, for the morning when the master got back to camp, his ten slaves had gone.…Wilson was next seen in Canada, making a safe trip with his ten. A reward was offered for his head, dead or alive, but they never got him.

When Abram Brooke moved to Marlboro, it seems that his involvement in antislavery moved up a notch, judging from the pages of the *Anti-Slavery Bugle*. That year, he was among the leaders of a rescue of a young girl in Salem, Ohio, from a train that had stopped there. The diary of Daniel Hise gives a good description of what occurred on the day of a Western Anti-Slavery Society meeting in Salem:

Attended the sessions of our Anti-slavery Meeting which were very interesting; at four o'clock it was announced that cars due from the east at six o-clock contained a slave; when our meeting adjourned to meet at the depot; as soon as the cars arrived a few friends (viz.) Ben Brown, Abram Brooke, Doc Thomas [Kersey G. Thomas], and Mr. Blackwell of Cincinnati,[195] *walked deliberately into them and asked a certain man in the vicinity of the supposed slave if she was really a slave; he answered that she belonged to him; no sooner than which they just picked the girl up and hurried her out of the car; his wife shrieked and he called murder as lustily as he knew how, but all to no purpose—he went on without her, but cursed and swore at a round rate about it. He gave us her clothes before leaving. In the evening a meeting was held to talk about the rescue, at which about fifty dollars was taken up, to defray the expense that might be incurred in clothing and educating her; she was also provided with a name: Abby Kelly Salem.*

The *Cleveland Herald* reported a more intense version of the events:

When the cars stopped, a big negro stepped into them, and accosting the girl, asked her if she was a slave. She made no reply but her mistress answered that she was. Thereupon the black ruffian seized her, and she, clinging to her mistress' neck, begged most piteously not to be torn away; but the black fellow violently tore her away, and in the effort bruised the lady's neck severely and carried the child out of the car on one arm, and flourished a revolver in the other hand, amid the plaudits of the excited crowd.[196]

Abram Brooke had gone to war over slavery, much like John Brown, though without a gun. He became a leader in the Disunionist movement,[197] and not surprisingly, he was an outspoken advocate of Brown's exploits. In 1858, fearing arrest for helping some nameless fugitive slave, he briefly went into exile, apparently in Canada:

I date from nowhere as I have no longer an abiding place in this great country. I am accused of the crime of attempting to assist a fellow being in the possession of those rights into which it has been said all men are born.[198]

Brooke was soon back home when it was learned that the story of his impending arrest was a rumor made up by his enemies. He died in 1867, hopefully somewhat content that the evil he had fought his entire had been ended.

Let us close this chapter on a happier time in his life, when he set out with Abram Allen and Valentine Nicholson and eight other abolitionists in 1843 for a trip to the anniversary meeting of the American Anti-Slavery Society in 1843. They were of early middle age—with Allen, the oldest, at forty-seven. Their eight fellow travelers were John O. Wattles, Amos Welsh, John and Maria McCowan, all of Harveysburg; Rebecca Nichols of Lloydsville, Belmont County, Ohio; Sara Dugdale and Elizabeth Borton of Green Plain; and Edwin Fussell of Pendleton, Indiana, nephew of the famed Chester County, Pennsylvania abolitionist Dr. Bartholomew Fussell. We defer to the pages of the *Standard*.[199]

On the evening of the day previous to the anniversary, a coach wagon, with four horses, drew up at the Anti-Slavery office. Reader…if you could have seen the company in that carriage, your heart would have leaped for joy. Those of our citizens and neighbors who did see it, could but blame themselves for cold and perverse indifference to the great work in hand; their zeal seemed like ice, compared with that which animated the pilgrim from Ohio and Indiana. Their arrival communicated a thrill of electricity, from the effects of which, may we never recover.

The wagon ought to be described, however, to enable our readers to see what righteous zeal can do, when it simply resolves to go forward. It is feet long, and wide; with a flat top and covering, on which to carry baggage. A hammock was slung at night, on which the men slept—the women resorting to houses in the neighborhood. Eight persons can be accommodated with lodging on board this "Great Western" land ship. The carriage is known by the name of Liberator, *because of its extensive service in aiding fugitives to liberate themselves from southern bondage. It picked up two on the voyage and gave them a considerable life freedomward. It was decorated with evergreens, some of which were distributed among the friends in this city, who preserve them as interesting memorials of the journey.*

The travelers carried their provisions with them; and as these consisted of Graham bread and apples, they considered it as quite luxurious, This they journeyed on, through pleasant and foul weather, to Concord,[200] where they…were to stop a couple of hours, [and] it was concluded to have an anti-slavery meeting [which] was addressed by John O. Wattles….The whole distance…was over seven hundred miles. Who would not gladly have shared the toils and pleasures of that journey?

Chapter 9

MYSTERIES OF THE UNDERGROUND RAILROAD

Wilbur Siebert's final book was titled *Mysteries of the Underground Railroad in Ohio*. It provides a summary of Underground Railroad activities and participants throughout most of the state. It is a bit remiss on the area that is the focus of this book. Neither Allen nor Nicholson is mentioned, although they did get a few lines in his first book, his major opus, *From Slavery to Freedom*—briefly listing the Liberator among noteworthy conveyances used to transport fugitives and describing Nicholson's technique of using burnt cork to darken the skin as a means of disguising a mulatto fugitive. Siebert collected so much information that much of it was never used in his books.

One aspect of the Underground Railroad that Siebert overemphasized was the secrecy involved. Of course, because of its illegality, its activities needed to be low profile, even secret at times. There was also the matter of violent opposition that slaveholders and even northerners who were proslavery would use to combat it. And combat it was, as has already been shown.

The antislavery newspapers were the efforts of extremely passionate people. Many people of the day likened them to fanatics, and many of these individuals went into the South and risked their lives to free slaves. Two were Reverends Charles Torrey and Abel Brown. Both died in their mid-thirties[201]—Torrey in prison after being caught rescuing slaves in the D.C. area and Brown from overwork and exhaustion after traveling thousands of miles, being assaulted by mobs and twice slipping across the border to rescue slaves. Brown did most of his work in the Albany area, where Torre readily supplied fugitives in numbers approaching three hundred, a figure he estimated himself. These men were journalists, as was James Birney, who was referenced at the Ohio Anti-Slavery's Society organizational meeting and who escaped a lynch mob in 1836 Cincinnati when he fortuitously was out of town. These men were courageous beyond belief; Brown actually published advertisements with names of slaves and their owners, taunting them.

This was certainly inadvisable, and both Torre and Brown met death early. Because it was so dangerous, few were brave enough to keep records. Only three such records of any considerable duration remain, so far as is known: William Still's *Journal*, which he used to write his book *The Underground Railroad: A Record*; Francis Jackson's *Treasurer's Account Book* of the Boston Vigilance Committee; and Sidney Howard Gay's *Record of Fugitives*, which covers two years of his work as the coordinator of one of the Underground Railroad networks in New York City.[202]

The mystery, not the facts, is what draws people, what makes it so fascinating, what brings out the detective in all of us. It's what hooked this author. On the other hand, serious historians disparage legends. They are like detectives in law enforcement looking for evidence and verifiable facts. Their business is not mythmaking. They become disappointed when they learn what they thought was true is merely an exaggeration, a contrivance or even sometimes a total fabrication.

This appears to be the case with Reverend William M. Mitchell, a man of color, who wrote *The Under-Ground Railroad*, the first book about the legendary network, published in England in 1860. He alleged to have lived in Ross and Fayette Counties, Ohio, from 1843 to 1855, moving finally to Washington Court House, where he said he was most active on the UGRR.[203]

Son of an American Indian mother and a free black father, his story is that he became an orphan and was indentured for twelve years, after which he became his employer's overseer and was obligated to assist in the slave trade. He not only punished slaves but also sold them away, and in the book, he expressed the horror he now felt for what he did. When he moved to Ross County, Ohio, in 1843, he atoned for it, he wrote, by dedicating his life to the Underground Railroad.

In one incident, in either Ross or Fayette County—it sounds like Ross, which had one of the state's largest black populations at that time—a Methodist minister reported that a fugitive slave was a member of his congregation.

Mitchell never gives names and renders pretty generic descriptions. Three slave catchers come for the man, and while they are leading him with a noose around his neck, a posse of two hundred crazed black men surged on them. Before they could be captured, the slave catchers cut this captive loose and raced away for their lives.

Mitchell said that his greatest period of activity in the Underground Railroad occurred after he moved to Washington Court House in Fayette County, Ohio. Here, one of the road's greatest conductors became a regular visitor to his home, or so Mitchell claims. A former slave, John Mason, whom this author has never found in any other document, had escaped to Canada and taken up the profession of slave rescuing. It just so happened that Mason was honoring Mitchell with his presence during his missions. Mason brought 265 runaways to Mitchell's home during a nineteen-month period, or so he said. That's not all. Mason claimed that he also aided as many as 1,300 fugitive slaves. Because of Mason's recklessness, Mitchell wrote, he was bound to be eventually captured. When they did capture him, they broke both his arms and sold him back into slavery. Yet lo and behold, his story had to have a happy ending—Mitchell received a letter from this most gifted of all slave rescuers that he was back in Canada, and that's all we hear of him. You would think that Mitchell would have looked him up when he moved to Canada in 1855. A man of his talent would certainly be well known, but Henry Bibb,[204] that greatest of all fugitive slave promoters during that time, never said a word about Mason.

Mitchell also used the stock, clichéd story of dressing up a fugitive as a woman to make the escape, and he not only mimicked "Box" Brown but also did him three times better, boxing up three men for shipment to freedom. Strange that of all the county histories, oral traditions and Siebert respondents, no one ever mentioned him.

In his book, Mitchell related additional stories about the Underground Railroad in which he was not involved, including one of a husband and wife who were reunited in Canada after twelve years when the woman came to a church looking for information about her husband and discovered that he was the pastor. He also related two stories that were told by respondents in the Siebert Collection and elsewhere, including the story of Louis, although he never gives his name or identifies any of the abolitionists who helped him, as we know that Levi Coffin was behind the rescue and sent him to the Nicholsons, who lived in adjacent Warren County.

Mitchell apparently left Ohio to work as missionary in Canada for the American Baptist Free Mission Society in 1855. He went on mission to

England to raise money for the society; his book was published there, and its sales were supposed to be used to raise money for his church. Knowing how star-struck the English abolitionists were over black American abolitionists,[205] they likely believed every word he said, or wrote, and published it without question. The *Bugle* reviewed it, but the article relied only on the book for its information. The fact that apparently no one in Ohio abolition knew him, even though he had left only five years before after allegedly living there for twelve years and being involved in some provocative incidents, is proof positive that his was a fable he slung for personal advancement. In 1863, while in England, Mitchell got into trouble for some dishonest statements and failure to pay bills. Not surprisingly, he faded into obscurity and died in 1879.[206]

SPRINGBORO

As early as 1816, and perhaps even earlier, the town of Springboro in the northeast corner of Warren County was aiding fugitives from slavery. Job Mullin, then more than ninety years old, gave his recollection to his son-in-law in response to Wilbur Siebert's inquiry:[207]

> *When about fifteen year of age, I was sent to Springboro and took a fugitive to our house on horseback, he riding behind me, it being in the night. At another time there was six persons, man, wife and children secreted in the loft over my loom shop two weeks. At the approach of anyone I would signal them by pounding on the floor with a cane….There were others harbored at my father's house at different times.*
>
> *I being married in 1829…and it being unlawful and many threats of burning the stations and property of those connected…did not take part further….The most active time to my knowledge was from 1816 to 1830.*

As has already been related, during the late 1830s and into 1840, a number of confrontations occurred between Springboro residents and slaveholders and slave traders who journeyed through the town with their slaves. Another reference in Beers's *History of Warren County* tells the story of an old fugitive named Hazard who had run away from near Lexington sometime in during the winter of 1837–38 and been caught by pursuers from Kentucky on the road to Springboro from Lebanon. When the townspeople found him tied up, they demanded his release. The men were brought before Judge Smith to determine the legality of the Kentuckians in their rendition[208] of him. The judge found in Hazard's favor, and he was allowed to continue on his way north to Canada.[209]

The trial that resulted after the Raines incident, which occurred in 1839, identified those who likely were most closely associated with the UGRR in the Springboro area,[210] including Cyrus Farr, William S. Bedford, the Potts, the Batemans (John and Warner) and Fred Wilson, the black man whom legend alleges brought ten men to Canada in 1836. Wilson also worked for the city's founder, the old Quaker Jonathan Wright. According to legend, Wright didn't like the idea of breaking the law but turned a blind's eye to Wilson hiding them on the Wright property.[211]

Others who clearly were involved included Ira Thomas, whose father had migrated from Adams County, Pennsylvania, where he aided fugitives from slavery who had crossed over the Maryland border.[212] Thomas, an agent until 1851 for the *Anti-Slavery Bugle*, remembered John Van Zandt[213] of Cincinnati, the model for Stowe's tragic character Van Trompe in *Uncle Tom's Cabin*, bringing fugitives to the Thomas home on one occasion. According to Thomas, the Ohio Supreme Court decision of 1841, which found that slaves knowingly brought into Ohio by their owners were free, encouraged more UGRR activity in Springboro until the passage of the Fugitive Slave Act of 1850 cooled it down again.

An interesting case of a slave, Lucinda, who had been purchased in Kentucky by Supreme Court judge John McLean and brought to his Ridgeville, Ohio residence near Springboro some years before was revealed by Abram Brooke in 1856 in the *Bugle*. Lucinda managed to escape after about one year of confinement to the house in 1838 and found assistance in Springboro, where it was decided that she had no reason to flee since she was now free in Ohio. This was made compelling because McLean—who was one of two judges to dissent in the Dred Scott Decision, which infamously decided that a "Negro has no rights that a white man is bound to respect"— did not pursue her.[214]

A number of UGRR conductors like Joel P. Davis, who said that "help was abundant"[215] in Springboro, listed it as an UGRR stop. However, Davis moved out of the area in 1846, and in conjunction with Ira Thomas's assertion of little activity after the passage of the Fugitive Slave Act of 1850, the record seems to indicate that the halcyon days of the UGRR in Springboro had passed by then. It is probably based on its early years of activity that credence is given to its legendary tunnels. In fact, with hostile towns to the west like Franklin and Dayton, which Davis said were avoided because of proslavery sentiments, it seems likely the route evolved eastward from Lebanon toward Xenia and up into Clark and Champaign Counties.

Xenia has long been legendary as a UGRR destination, and much of its reputation lies with it being the site of the first exclusively black college in 1856, when the UGRR was at its height. David Monroe, the Xenia cabinet maker, was a regular recipient of fugitives from Abram Allen, and in several letters from Greene County recipients, other local participants are identified. In the Cyrus Little letter to Daniel Orcutt, he identified seven UGRR agents, including himself, in Greene County.[216]

However, the road through the county was getting more contentious as the years progressed toward the Civil War. On May 25, 1854, James T. McCord kidnapped a free black man, Eli Cook of Waynesville, who was walking along the road near Xenia. His intention was to sell him into slavery. During several scuffles to secure him, McCord murdered him by hitting him over the head with a club. The fracas was witnessed by several people, and he was convicted of second-degree murder.[217]

TUNNELS

Tunnels, tunnels and more tunnels. They are ubiquitous in the legends of the UGRR, and most of them are apocryphal. When someone talks about the UGRR in Springboro, it is always associated with the nine tunnels that were located under the streets, leading to the cellars of the abolitionists. Old-timers told many tales of actually seeing them as children. But no stories of their actual use exist. They are like the quilt fable, a more recent relic of UGRR lore in which people have become emotionally invested. Today, the tunnels have all collapsed, and until some evidence that they were used can be found, it will be just that—a nice fable that helps preserve the UGRR's memory in Springboro history.

When Dr. Jesse Harvey founded Harveysburg in 1829, there already were dedicated abolitionists living in the Caesar Creek area, like Thomas Wales, the father of Jane Nicholson and Nancy Butterworth. However, his progressive views fit right in, and from the start, his son said he was involved in the UGRR and that his house was "a special depot where hundreds passed through our town."[218] He also established Warren County's first antislavery society in 1836, which had seventeen members at that time.[219]

But the Harveys, Jesse and his wife, Elizabeth, had more conventional concerns. They energies were devoted to the education of blacks for whom Ohio communities had no provision. Elizabeth opened the first grammar school for blacks in Harveysburg in 1831, and Jesse started an academy or high school in 1837 with the hope of integrating it. That year, Stephen Wall, a slaveholder from North Carolina, brought his five children, who also were his slaves, to the Harveys to be educated. It is thought that their arrival originated his idea of integrating his high school. But it met with strong opposition in the community, and he gave in to their wishes.

In 1847, the Harveys left for the Kansas Territory to work at a Shawnee Indian mission.[220] Greater involvement in antislavery activities then developed as a result of the Nicholsons' influence. In 1851, an antislavery society for the counties of Clinton and Warren was formed in Harveysburg on November 30. Nicholson was secretary and J.G. Stevenson president. A Harveysburg wagon maker, Stevenson was for a time married to Nicholson's brother-in-law, Thomas, until her untimely death. Among its twenty-nine members were Jane Nicholson Abram Allen, Abram Brooke and three of the Wall children, who by then were nearing adulthood.[221] An interesting sidenote to the Harveys' story is the success of the Wall children, all of whom were freed and given a substantial inheritance by their slaveholding father. All but one moved to Oberlin, and three of them furthered their education there. Caroline met and married John Mercer Langston, and Orindatus, or "Datis," was one of the thirty-seven who carried out the famed Oberlin-Wellington rescue in 1858.[222]

The Harveysburg UGRR was undoubtedly coordinated by Nicholson. Robert Carroll, who sometimes transported fugitives there for Henry T. Butterworth, wrote this interesting comment:

> *At Harveysburg, where the citizens were generally sympathizers, the Negroes were permitted some publicity, and the whole party openly sat down to breakfast at the hospitable board of Valentine Nicholson. It was my first meal with the despised caste, but I was conscious of no loss of self-respect.*

Waynesville is similar to Harveysburg in that it, too, was a Quaker community, and while there are legends associated with Seth Haines and Moses McKay, who moved to Waynesville and brought with him his twenty-two slaves whom he freed, there is little documentation of their UGRR involvement. There are also legends related to the use of caves and tunnels there. More reliable are two sources that confirm occasional aid to fugitives given by abolitionist publisher Achilles Pugh after he moved there in 1854.[223] Also, Thomas Miller, who lived east of Springboro, said he once took "five or six" fugitives to Waynesville.[224] Just to the south in Lebanon, attorney R.G. Corwin, who was one of the attorneys who represented the abolitionists in the Raines case, wrote that "fugitives were there almost daily" between 1840 and 1850.[225] And Amy Clark, a former slave who lived in Cincinnati and moved to Canada in 1835, said that her husband delivered fugitives to Lebanon but did not indicate where they were sent.[226] An undated letter in the Siebert Collection from Mrs. E.S. Shepardson notes that "Waynesville… has probably sheltered more fugitives and furthered them on their way than any other place in the state of Ohio."[227] So, it's likely that some fugitives made their way to Waynesville.

On the other hand, there were those in Waynesville who strongly disapproved of the abolitionists. Abram Brooke wrote about an incident that took place there after the Raines incident. It occurred in the fall of 1840 when another slaveholder was passing along the same road as Raines. The abolitionists had the slaveholder arrested on the charge of kidnapping, based on an 1837 Ohio law, but Judge Smith of Lebanon dismissed the charges and released him. Expecting that the abolitionists might try to take the slaves by force, Brooke wrote:

> [The] *citizens of Waynesville and vicinity actually took arms and stood a volunteer body guard over the captives to prevent the enforcement of their own laws. And when the slaveholders saw fit to move on their journey, this guard marched with them to the verge of the county to protect their right to human property.*[228]

One of the problems that we have today regarding the assessment of the Underground Railroad for both Harveysburg and Waynesville was the creation of Caesar Creek Lake in 1978. It destroyed many remnants that could have borne testimony to the UGRR in those towns. The truth about houses like those of Haines and McKay and the use of tunnels probably will never be known.

Such are the mysteries of the Underground Railroad.

Chapter 10

THE SAD SONG OF THE UNDERGROUND RAILROAD

Trudging past Clinton and Warren Counties, the pilgrims of freedom could have been taken on a number of routes. The Liberator's primary itinerary conveyed them to Port William, where their conductor took them to Selma, Green Plain Meeting in Clark County. Onward through Mechanicsburg, they sidestepped Columbus and went up to William Cratty's in Delaware, Ohio, and then from Cratty to the Alum Creek Settlement and the Benedicts, a virtual ring of abolitionist fire. The fugitives also could have gone through Washington Court House, which was an intersection of routes from Adams through Highland Counties and the Warren-Clinton route, into Columbus. But as some of the respondents who conveyed fugitives in the rural counties noted, urban areas were avoided because of the greater likelihood of detection.[229]

Examinations of accounts by these deliverers of freedom indicate that Columbus was an alternate route, and numbers associated with the workers there support this. It also began relatively late in its UGRR involvement, starting in the mid-1830s, in comparison with areas south of it when river towns like Ripley were aiding fugitives in the first decade of the century.

This is not to say that those in Columbus were any less passionate in their support for fugitives and an end to slavery. Columbus was a small city during the antebellum period. Its population in 1850 was 17,882 compared with Cincinnati's 115,405. But it had nearly five times as many people of color per capita.[230] One of Columbus's UGRR workers was John T. Ward:

John T. Ward.

*I first came to know of the U.G.R.R....
when I was 22 years old here in Columbus
[1842]. Shepherd Alexander (colored) had a
team which used in conveying. He lived in
the south end of town, between Livingston
Ave. and Columbia Street, on the east side of
High Street.*

*The probabilities are that there were stations
south of us—particularly Bloomingburg in
connection with Washington C.H....[and]
Chillicothe, looked after by colored men....
Richard Chancelor and Robert Chancelor, his
son, John Fidler, Jesse Fidler, and Andrew
Redmond* [Chillicothe was another area
often avoided according to those who transported fugitives].[231]

*Connected with the Columbus station were David Jenkins, John Bookel,
Thomas Washington, Lewis Washington, Sr.* [father of Thomas],
*Rev. James Poindexter, though he never went out with us much—Wm.
Washington, Wm Ferguson, Jeremiah Freeland, and others.*

*The next station was near Worthington—just this side—a regular
rendezvous. Some went there that didn't even hit us....The station was at
the residence of Mr. Jason Bull. I think Delaware was the next station,
and after that I cannot say.*[232]

Another factor in the avoidance of more urbanized centers like Columbus
was the anti-abolition and racial prejudice that existed. For example, on
December 27, 1843, when David Jenkins inaugurated his *Palladium of Liberty*,
he penned this scathing rebuke of the white citizenry:

*The prejudice, of which we are the objects, is the most vindictive, cruel, and
unprecedented of the age, in an enlightened and Christianized country....
Whilst foreigners, after a short sojourn in our country, have a voice in
electing our rulers, we, are forbidden by it, to manifest our interest in the
welfare of our country, by depositing our vote in the ballot box. By it, our
children are shut out from the common schools, for no other cause than, that
God has enclosed their minds in forms tinged with African blood.*[233]

Jenkins was a construction contractor, skilled in painting, glazing and
plastering. He was one of Ohio's leading black activists during the antebellum

Left: David Jenkins; *Right*: Reverend James Poindexter. *Courtesy Ohio History Center.*

period and one of the leaders in the state's Colored Convention movement, being appointed president at its 1851 convention in Columbus.[234]

Reverend James Poindexter, the spiritual leader of the Columbus black community during the antebellum period, was born in Richmond, Virginia, in 1819. His father was white, and his mother a mix of white, black and American Indian ancestry. His mother died when he was four, and he became a barber's apprentice at age ten. At age eighteen, he married and moved to Columbus in 1838.[235] In 1840, he became pastor of the Baptist church, which became known as the Anti-Slavery Baptist Church. He said he became aware of the UGRR in the city from the start and that his connection with it continued until the end of slavery. He identified the same men as Jenkins as being its main agents and singled out Lewis Washington as an imposing figure with the strength of five average men and who, like Alexander, was a teamster, supplying horses and wagons. According to Poindexter, the coordinating conductor of the entire operation was Methodist minister Jason Bull in Clintonville, who was the regular recipient of fugitives.[236]

Born in Vermont circa 1793, Bull moved to Clintonville with his family when he was about twenty.[237] Though a Methodist minister, he always wore the traditional wide-brimmed hat of the Quakers, which was the denomination of his ancestors.[238] He and his brothers began to harbor fugitives sometime in the early 1830s. Behind their homestead on High Street was, and still is, a deep ravine cut by a creek along which fugitives could move unnoticed. Next to it was built Bull's church, the Clintonville Chapel. Amason Webster was the chapel's superintendent:[239]

> *I knew all about the slaves, wrote Webster....They stored them in Clinton Chapel often....The back part was about four feet deep from the joist down, with a window at the back and a door in front, and there we stowed fuel and slaves. The Church was built 1837 or 1838. Before that time they were stored in the barn.*[240]

Cynthia Spurgeon, Jason Bull's daughter, gave her recollections. She conveyed the stress associated with the Underground Railroad in more populated areas where the likelihood of being detected was more probable:

> *We used to keep potatoes in the rear part of the church; I presume father did put the slaves in there. I used to be sent over to the barn across the way,*

Clintonville Chapel. *Courtesy Tom Calarco.*

with a little egg basket filled with provisions, and I would take this over as though I were going to gather eggs; and when there, would call to the slaves, and hand up the provisions to them.

A colored man and his wife came one night and the man was terribly scared, for he was sure he had seen his master and another man in the city....The man was dressed up as a driver, and the wife was dressed up pretty fine with a heavy green veil over her face. Father sat alongside her in a canopied-top carriage with a high collar on. Two men did ride by with the palmetto hats on [the hats worn by the slaveholders], *but the darkey acted natural, though father said it was difficult for him.* [They] *stopped at Worthington but finally got to Gardner's.*[241]

Edward Sebring began working with Jason Bull when he was only seventeen years old:

In 1856, I was called upon to escort three colored persons to Ozem Gardner's. I supposed I went twenty times with colored persons...

I was a boy and Uncle Jason used to say to me, to say nothing about carrying off the darkies; that these people were looking for their liberty, and that [we] *were trying to help them to it.*

When I was first asked to carry those niggers away, I felt that my dignity had been assailed. I had been raised a Democrat and had been taught that all abolitionists were very bad, and tampering with niggers very bad: but after seeing the backs of these poor fellows I felt differently, and went with pleasure. At the time High Street was a plank road as far as Worthington, and from there on nothing but a mud road. We used to have difficulty on account of the deep ruts, especially after night. The alarm that I would give at Ozem Gardner's was three raps on the door. After the alarm a light would be lighted in the house and the door opened and they would be taken in and cared for and then put in the barn.[242]

James Ferguson, who also lived on High Street in Clintonville, harbored fugitives. There was a hazel thicket on his place down by the creek, and in this thicket was an opening of a tunnel that led to his basement. One time, Ferguson's ten-year-old grandson, unbeknownst to him, took four fugitives in his father's false-bottom wagon to the thicket. On his way, two horsemen stopped him and asked him what was in the hay, another instance demonstrating the greater hazards on transportation in more populated areas. The boy said there was nothing but hay, as he had been led to believe. But one of the men took the pitchfork that was in the wagon and jabbed into the hay. With the slaves being in the false bottom maintaining their composure, he detected nothing, and the boy was allowed to go on his way.[243]

Bull's collaborator, Ozem Gardner, who became interested in antislavery in 1836, lived about seven miles from Bull, just north of Worthington. He came to Ohio from the Cooperstown, New York area in 1817 when he was twenty. Three years later, he bought the homestead where he would remain the rest of his life.[244]

The first recorded incident in which he was involved occurred in 1835. It may have led to the formation of the Worthington Anti-Slavery Society on March 28, 1836, of which Gardner and Ansel Mattoon, another UGRR agent, were members.[245] Four slaves, a mother and her children, two boys and a girl, were rescued by residents of Columbus's black community from a slave owner on the way to Missouri while he was camped on the banks of the Scioto River. They were hidden in Columbus and then transported to the farm of Gardner, who brought them to the Alum Creek residence of William Benedict, where they remained several days. The slaveholder traced them there, went to Alum Creek accompanied by two men from Worthington and spotted two of the children in the yard of William, who was attending a church meeting. They attempted to abduct the children, but before they could get too far, the Quakers were alerted and stopped them. Justice of the Peace Barton Whipple was summoned, and he charged the men with kidnapping and told them they were liable to a heavy fine and jail time. William, however, suggested dropping the charges if the men agreed to leave, berating the slaveholder because one of the boys was his son, and the matter was concluded.

Two of Gardner's sons wrote to Wilbur Siebert:

> *Sometime my father would take them into the house but most generally put them in the barn. Sometime he would take in a big wagon covered up: sometimes in an ancient carriage and generally after night,* wrote *Wilson Gardner.*
>
> *They often brought fugitives…from Bull's to fathers by the State Road,* wrote *Joseph.…They often brought fugitives to Blendon* [Westerville] *to throw them off the track…to Sharp's. Garret Sharp was the old man.…He had six or seven sons all abolitionists.…The Mattoon's also received Negroes.*[246]

Ozem Gardner House. *Courtesy Tom Calarco.*

According to 1880 *History of Pickaway and Franklin Counties*, Gardner is credited with aiding more than two hundred fugitives. Both his sons and the county history indicated that he usually brought the fugitives to the Alum Creek Settlement near Mount Gilead.

JERRY PHINNEY

In 1846, the kidnapping of a black man in Columbus stirred the city like perhaps no other incident during the antebellum period. Jerry Phinney had resided there for some fifteen years and was married with five children. He was well known in the community as a cook and waiter at the city's public houses. Unbeknownst to the public was that Jerry was a fugitive slave from Frankfort, Kentucky, owned by the Long family. His escape had been facilitated as a result of being leased in 1830 to a gambler, Allagier, who brought him to Cincinnati, a violation of the lease agreement. When

Phinney's owner learned of this, she demanded Phinney be returned, to which Allagier complied. However, during his time in Cincinnati, Phinney acquired the knowledge he needed to make his escape. When he returned to Frankfort, he said he needed to return to Cincinnati to get some of his things that he had left behind. Once in Cincinnati, he disappeared into the black community, finally moving to Columbus.

Although years had passed, Phinney worried about the possibility of someday being discovered. In 1845, he went to a lawyer, who advised him to write to the Longs, requesting his emancipation. By this time, his owner had died and the family had scattered. Only a daughter-in-law, Bathsheba Long, remained. Being in debt, she was not about to easily give up her "property." A neighbor, Alexander Forbes, offered to track Phinney, and he arranged a ruse with one of Columbus's justices of the peace, William Henderson. He also a hired another Kentuckian, Jacob Armitage, to pose as a bridegroom who needed help carrying luggage to the JOP's office, where his bride-to-be awaited for their wedding ceremony.

On March 27, the plan was executed. Phinney brought the luggage with the help of a boy. Waiting for them with Henderson were Forbes, Sheriff Henry Henderson, David Potts, Daniel Zinn and John Stephenson, who pounced on Phinney, handcuffed him, tied him up and placed a gag over his mouth. A legal proceeding followed, after which Henderson remanded him to Forbes, the representative of Long, as a fugitive slave. He was placed in Zinn's carriage and hurried off to Kentucky. The boy who had accompanied Phinney was detained until after Zinn, the Kentuckians and Phinney had left town. When he was released, he called out the alarm and a posse was organized. They chased them to Xenia, where it was expected that the kidnappers would board the train, but were too late; they continued on to Cincinnati, the full one hundred or so miles—all to no avail, as the kidnappers were able to cross into Kentucky on a mail boat. Later, it was learned that they had delivered Phinney to the warden of the Frankfort penitentiary, Newton Craig, who met them in Cincinnati and took custody of Phinney.[247] Craig would become notorious for his dalliance with slave rescuer Delia Webster, and his lashings of her accomplice, Calvin Fairbank. It was reported that Craig paid Forbes and Armitage $300 each for the delivery of Phinney.[248]

In the following days, Governor Bartley of Ohio contacted the governor of Kentucky and demanded the reclamation of Forbes and Armitage on the charge of kidnapping, as Henderson and his Ohio accomplices were arrested. A large public meeting was held in Columbus at the Town Center

Methodist-Episcopal Church. Reverend Granville Moody and Samuel Galloway lashed out against the kidnappers, and the boisterous crowd clamored for the rescue of Jerry.

Shortly after the Kentucky kidnappers were tried in Kentucky, the state governor refusing to extradite. They were tried and found not guilty under a Kentucky state law that absolved all abductions of fugitive slaves, as proof was shown that under Kentucky law, Phinney was the slave of Bathsheba Long.

The litigation dragged on, and Jerry remained in prison. It wasn't until September that the trial of the other kidnappers began. All were tried at the same time. It was a quick affair, and all were found innocent but the JOP, Henderson, who was remanded to jail. While Henderson was sent to jail, Phinney was released from prison, as noted in the *Columbus Post* and re-published in the *New York Evening Post*:

> *Jerry Phinney…is now restored to his family. He is quite emaciated.… Five hundred dollars were paid to secure his release.… The sum was paid by our citizens under the impression that he could not otherwise be restored to his suffering family.*[249]

Eight months later, when Henderson's case was thrown out on a writ of error by the Ohio Supreme Court, he became a free man. It is not known if Jerry Phinney was still alive, as the historical record states that he died soon after his release from prison.[250]

While Columbus may not have been a major terminal on the UGRR, it did have a strong contingent of abolitionists, both black and white. The state colored conventions in Ohio owed much to the influence of its black community, and its representatives at these eight conventions between the years 1843 and 1857 were largely the same persons identified by Ward as agents for the UGRR. Also contributing to the work of these conventions were the Langston brothers, Charles and John, the former residing in Columbus from about 1850 to 1856. Charles was one of the leaders of the city's Anti-Fugitive Slave Law meeting that took place shortly after its passage.

"We pledge ourselves, it resolved, "that no fugitive from labor, or person claimed as such shall ever be taken from our midst…and we advise all colored persons to go continually prepared, that we may be ready at any moment to offer defense in behalf of their liberty."[251]

Reverend Poindexter, who was a regular attendee at these conventions, seems to have been a liaison between the black and white communities, judging by the many leadership positions he held over the years in civic organizations and his acknowledgement of the interrelationship of whites and blacks in the UGRR. In legal matters, since there were no black lawyers—the first black lawyer in Ohio was John Mercer Langston, who passed the bar exam in 1855—black abolitionists were dependent on white abolitionists.

In addition to the Bull family, the leading white abolitionists were Dr. James Coulter, James Westwater and Louis Van Slyke. It was Coulter who proposed the establishment of a newspaper in Columbus devoted to the principles of antislavery. Called the *Ohio Columbian*, it published both news of interest and articles related to slavery and antislavery. It had two editors during its run from 1853 to 1856, Lewis L. Rice and Allen Matters Gangewer, both experienced journalists, and was sometimes referred to as "Chase's paper" because Rice was then Ohio governor Salmon Chase's personal secretary. Coulter and Van Slyke played a major role in the rescue of the slave Rosetta Armistead in 1855.[252]

Rosetta was a sixteen-year-old mulatto under five feet tall owned by Louisville minister Reverend Henry M. Dennison. She was being sent to Virginia to assist his daughter. She was entrusted with a Dr. Miller to take her there. They set out on a steamer up the Ohio River to take them to Wheeling, Virginia. However, their plans were set back by ice jams, and they were forced to get off in Cincinnati and seek passage by rail. Miller was apprehensive about bringing a slave into a free state, and when faced with staying over in Zanesville or Columbus, he chose the latter because he thought the abolitionists would pose less trouble there. Apparently, they were spotted by some colored women, who reported their belief that a slave was staying in town. Through Judge Joseph R. Swan, a writ of habeas corpus was obtained, likely by Charles Langston, on the grounds that she was now free, being brought into a free state.[253] The judge declared her so and appointed Van Slyke as her guardian. It wasn't long before Reverend Dennison came to Columbus seeking to reclaim and went to Van Slyke's residence, asking to speak to her and learn if she really wanted to be free. The conversation that was transcribed from Van Slyke's testimony during the trial held to determine her legal status is revealing:

> *"What do you think of this?" Dennison said. "They have got you in a fine fix."*
>
> *She didn't answer.*
>
> *"You know now that you are free, you will not be able to see your parents or little Bessie* [Dennison's daughter], *or any of your friends back home."*

Dennison continued trying to coax her back.

"And you will have to work harder in freedom. Look at what happened to Aunt Sally, how hard she has had to work as a free woman. Nor you will wear the fine clothes that I am able to provide."

There was silence.

"Now, Rosetta, I leave the matter for you to decide, and it shall be as you say."

Rosetta hesitated, then finally said meekly, "I desire to be free."[254]

Thereafter, Van Slyke placed Rosetta with the family of Coulter. Several days later, two men arrived at Coulter's with a warrant issued by a U.S. commissioner to take custody of Rosetta. Coulter balked and said he needed to consult with others before acquiescing to the warrant. As he went to his neighbors to give the alarm, the officers hurried off in a carriage with Rosetta. Fortunately, Van Slyke and Dr. W.E. Ide managed to arrive at the train station before it left for Cincinnati with Rosetta aboard and had wired ahead to Salmon Chase, who initiated a writ of habeas corpus that greeted the officers when they arrived and brought Rosetta before Judge Parker in the Court of Common Pleas.

The case hinged on the question of whether Rosetta actually was a fugitive slave who had escaped into Ohio, and if she were, then her owner would have the right to reclaim. But Chase and his team of lawyers, including John Joliffe and Rutherford B. Hayes, argued that she had been brought knowingly and willfully into a free state, which should automatically confer her freedom. The judge ruled this to be the case.

Nevertheless, Dennison, who was present, demanded that the case be tried in a federal court. He said it should have jurisdiction and that he would make an effort to have the case brought before it. In doing so, he made an apology for slavery whose rationale is such a classic denial of responsibility used by those in support of slavery that it deserves recounting:

It seems to be supposed that everyone who holds a fellow creature in bondage is unworthy of respect, and of a villainous heart.

Now, sir, when I see some ten or fifteen millions of the intelligent portion of the people of this republic, men of character and respectability, and high position in life, educated some in the North and some in the South, men of extensive reading as any of those before the court, men who would just as little violate the principles of true morality as any of these—I say, sir, that in sight of all this, it should, at least, raise a doubt as to whether those who hold property in slaves really merit the abuse that is so frequently heaped upon them.[255]

Dennison's pleas made no traction with the judge, who ordered Rosetta to be returned to Van Slyke and added an order of protection because of the likelihood that a federal marshal would try to take custody of her again. And in fact, minutes after the trial was concluded, U.S. Marshal H.H. Robinson delivered a warrant for Rosetta to appear before U.S. Commissioner John L. Pendery.

The case now focused on states' rights versus the federal government, an issue that factored in many of the fugitive slave cases, especially because many of the northern states had passed "personal liberty laws"[256] that interfered with the federal fugitive slave laws. It was this very issue of states' rights versus the federal government that precipitated the Civil War, only in that case, it was the Southern states' demanding their right to hold human beings as property. The attorney for Dennison, a Mr. Wolfe, prophesied that this would occur at the hearing:

There will be bloody times hereabouts when the fanaticism prevalent on this side of the Ohio has proceeded a few steps further. The time is approaching when, if these outrages on the rights of Kentucky persisted scenes would be enacted that the eyes of humanity would be pained to gaze upon.[257]

Rosetta was returned to Van Slyke, and the abolitionists had won. Even better for Rosetta, a wealthy New England woman had taken an interest in her case and offered to make a home for her and provide with the best education and life possible. Interesting that along with this good news for antislavery, there was this report in the *Ohio Columbian*:

While the "right" of Rosetta was undergoing the forms of trial, in the Cincinnati courts, there were ten of the human species passed near that city, on the road to Canada. They consisted of two women and their five children, and two young men, and one boy 12 or 14 years of age. The mothers and their children were bright mulattoes; one of the women was the daughter of a slaveholder, and so white was she, that any person, without a close inspection, would take her to be of pure Anglo-Saxon blood. On the question being asked what induced them to leave their Southern homes, they replied that their masters had a few months since sold to the South their husbands, and as they had not friends or relatives left, they determined on the hazardous undertaking of escaping from a lain of chains.[258]

The reader may wonder about the italicized sentence. It sticks out as inappropriate in our modern era, but it is not unusual. In many accounts by abolitionists and their discussion of fugitive slaves, there is this obsession with those who were almost white or even whiter than some whites. We are back to the conundrum of color that plagues our deep psychological core. You feel inclined to ask writers of such sentences if they are implying that it's even worse for a white person to be a slave than for one of color.

A poignant story concerns Dr. James Coulter.[259] It's similar to the story about Fernando and Sophia Kelton, who adopted a fugitive slave girl just before the Civil War and whose house is now a museum on 586 East Town Street. Coulter's house was actually in the same neighborhood. Coulter's son, Ernest, wrote to Siebert in 1935 about his father. He said they had two hiding places for fugitives: a haymow in a barn and an attic that could be reached only through a hidden cubbyhole. He said his father had taken such pity on a poor fugitive slave boy who arrived one night with nothing but overalls that he "adopted" and raised the boy and put him through college. His name was John Brown, and he became an assistant attorney general in the state of Kansas.[260]

After the war and the passing of the Fifteenth Amendment, which gave people of color the right to vote, one of the former slaves whom Coulter had rescued went to the voting place at the old Gay Street engine house. There he was prevented from voting by a mob. His father interceded, and in the melee that followed, he was struck on the head. It was an injury, said his son, that plagued him for the rest of his life.

As is said of many historic structures, "if the walls could only talk." Whether you are a serious historian or amateur sleuth who loves to send your imagination into the past, you understand the meaning of this cliché and the feeling you get when you enter an old, historic house where important events occurred. Many people feel that way about the UGRR. It could be said of the Hanby House, a modest museum on the Otterbein College campus in Westerville, Ohio, just north of Columbus.[261]

William Hanby, a minister and one of the founders of Otterbein College, moved here with his family in 1854. An elder in the United Brethren in Christ denomination, he grew up as an indentured servant and vowed to never turn away from others who were oppressed like he had been. He had been aiding fugitives from slavery since the late 1830s, when he lived in Rushville, Ohio, collaborating with Dr. Simon Hyde.

Above: Kelton House; *Below*: Hanby House. *Courtesy Tom Calarco.*

Reverend William Hanby. *Courtesy Ohio History Center.*

In 1842, he became involved in an incident that would later be recorded for posterity. A fugitive slave, Joseph Selby, came to Rushville and found his way to the Hanby barn. He was deathly sick and Dr. Hyde was summoned, but there was little that could be done but make him comfortable. During his last hours, he revealed the story of his beloved Nelly Gray, who had been sold and sent south the day before they were to be married. Selby had escaped in the hopes of earning enough money to purchase her freedom.

Hanby told the story to his children. His oldest, Ben, followed in his footsteps, becoming a teacher and minister and helping in the UGRR business. He also had another talent. He was a composer, and at a young age, he began writing songs. It is believed that he gave his first performance of his ballad "Darling Nelly Gray" at the Hanby house in 1856. At the time, Otterbein College president Lewis Day, who also participated in the UGRR, lived next door.[262]

A barn behind the Hanby house was where they hid the runaways. According to legend, the Hanbys had a special signal to alert their collaborators that runaways were present. They would put a vase of roses in their front window, with the number of roses indicating the number of runaways. Dinner was served to the fugitives in the Hanby house, and it was Ben's job to cover the windows to hide them. It was also his job to lead the slaves out of the barn during the night to the false-bottom wagon of toolmaker Thomas Alexander, who would usually take them to Mount Vernon, about thirty miles north.

Meanwhile, Ben had sent "Darling Nelly Gray" to a publisher in Boston who published it without his knowledge. He only learned about it when his sister heard it sung in Columbus. It became a huge success, and an arrangement for band music became popular. The Christy Minstrels used it as their featured song, and it became a favorite in England. It even would become popular in the Confederacy. General George Pickett loved it and had his band play it in Chambersburg on the way to the Battle of Gettysburg.[263]

Ben Hanby. *Courtesy Ohio History Center.*

But fate would not be so kind to the Hanbys. In 1867, while working for a music publisher in Chicago, Ben contracted tuberculosis and died. Four years later, the Great Chicago Fire destroyed the documentation that proved Ben's authorship of many of his compositions, and as time passed, even "Darling Nelly Gray" was attributed to Stephen Foster.

In 1870, William Hanby lost his house because of debts incurred as a result of loans he had co-signed for others in need, and he was persecuted because of his outspoken views on temperance. He died penniless and crippled in 1880, living in a rented house. It does not seem fair that good men should meet such unhappy endings. It does not seem fair that slaveholders could separate family members and loved ones for the sake of their profit. But this was a sad song of the Underground Railroad that was sung time and time again.

One night I went to see her
She's gone, the neighbors say
The white man bound her with his chain.
They have taken her to Georgia
For to wear her life away
As she toils in the cotton and cane.

Oh my poor Nelly Gray,
They have taken you away,
And I'll never see my darling any more;
I am sitting by the river
And I'm weeping all the day,
For you've gone from the old Kentucky shore.

Chapter 11

THE ABOLITIONIST
RING OF FIRE

A s earlier suggested, heavier fugitive slave traffic skirted the Columbus area, which was a consequence of an organic abolitionist ring of fire manned by some of the UGRR's most dedicated souls. They included Udney Hyde in Mechanicsburg, William Cratty of Delaware and the Benedicts of the Alum Creek Settlement in Morrow County, which was one of the state's most inspired UGRR communities.

Up through Greene County, quite a few UGRR agents were available.[264] This led them up to the UGRR of the Green Plain Meeting, where the Dugdales played a leadership role;[265] to the abolitionist town of South Charleston, a few miles farther north; and finally on to Mechanicsburg. According to Beers's history of Champaign County, the routes through Mechanicsburg were established in the early 1840s, when the traffic through nearby Springfield and Urbana had become well known and was frequently watched.[266]

Among the town's earliest operators was Joseph "Jakie" Ware. He hid fugitives in his basement, which locals referred to as the "catacombs" because of the way it was arranged to hide spaces and hidden rooms. Ware became involved in abolition after a trip into the South, where he witnessed a slave auction. He transported fugitives in his wagon under loads of hay. One time, when slave catchers were nearby, he let his young daughter, Anna, drive the wagon to avoid suspicion. One of the places that Ware frequently took fugitives was to a farm operated by Pearl Howard called "Lazy Man's Rest." Here the slaves were kept in a false-walled vault

Jakie Ware. *Courtesy Ohio History Center.*

in the cellar with a hiding place at the end of a long tunnel. Other UGRR workers in Mechanicsburg were Levi Rathburn, David Rutan, Charles Taylor and Alexander Doty, as well as a good number of others in the surrounding area.[267]

The good works picked up, however, when a goodly man of moral fiber became involved.

UDNEY HYDE

Udney H. Hyde did much more of personal labor than any other one man at this point, to effectually further on their way more than half a thousand slaves. He could out swear any man in Champaign County, and, if any man in the world could beat him, his vocabulary would contain nothing else. He was fearless, shrewd and bold, [and] a good horseman.[268]

Born in Vermont, Hyde settled in Mechanicsburg, Ohio, where he was a farmer, clock peddler and blacksmith. It was said that his participation in the Underground Railroad began in 1851 after observing that when young lambs were separated from their mothers, the black lambs mourned for their offspring as much as the white. It led to his realization that aiding slaves to escape would be "keeping the laws of God."

119

For Hyde's first mission, on September 20, 1851,[269] he assisted seven runaways, all of whom stayed the night at Hyde's residence. The next morning, he loaded them in his wagon and covered them up with hay. One of the runaways was a free black man named Penny from Ripley, Ohio. He had wanted to marry a slave girl owned by a Baptist preacher in Kentucky. He made a bargain to work for the preacher for a year to pay for her emancipation. However, at the year's end, the preacher reneged on the deal. He gave Penny forty dollars and told him to leave his property. The following Saturday night, Penny returned and carried off the others with him—his sweetheart, her sister, her brother-in-law and another man. They vowed that they would become free or die, and if anyone tried to turn back, Penny would shoot them. When they reached the banks of the Ohio River, they were confronted by slave catchers, and there was an exchange of shots that wounded a slavecatcher and a slave. Nevertheless, they crossed the river, leaving the wounded man with friends in Ripley, and moved up through the UGRR to Mechanicsburg.

Hyde's boldness disarmed his adversaries. During a trip to Ripley to get castings for his blacksmith shop, he retrieved a slave of light complexion. On the way to Mechanicsburg, he realized that the roads were under close surveillance, so on the trip to William Cratty's in Delaware, he dressed the slave in his wife's clothing with a bonnet and veil and headed there on two horses. Everything went well until they approached Bellepointe along the Scioto River, when he heard the sound of hoofbeats. The girl looked back and thought it was her master. Hyde told her to keep jerking on the right rein to make the horse prance so as to keep her back to the approaching riders. Fortunately, they were nearing their destination, the farm of a Quaker preacher, and he gave the woman directions.

"No matter what happens," he said, "pay no attention, just keep sauntering on down the road." As the slave catchers closed in, Hyde called out to the runaway, addressing her as if she were his wife. When they rounded a bend, the runaway sped off the road through a clearing directly to the Quaker's farm with Hyde following. The slave catchers continued their pursuit, and as the runaway reached the farmhouse, Hyde turned his horse around. He galloped his horse toward them. They both came to a halt.

"God damn you! If you fellows ever follow me and my wife again," Hyde shouted, "I'll shoot you! You hear me, like a God damn dog." The resolution in Hyde's steely eyes must have frightened them because they turned around and left Hyde and the girl alone.

False-bottom wagon. *Courtesy Tom Calarco, Levi Coffin House.*

Another time, while transporting a load of runaways concealed in his wagon, he was asked by a posse of slave catchers what was under the hay. Hyde responded, "Niggers, God damn, you!" Startled, they let him proceed.

Hyde's guile and ability to disguise his emotions were what enabled him to successfully transport so many runaways without one ever being returned to slavery. For instance, a runaway frantically knocked on his door seeking shelter from slave catchers close behind. At once, Hyde hid the runaway in his false-bottom wagon and headed back in the direction the runaway had come. After a time, they came upon the wagon of slaveholder whom Hyde knew.

"Here comes a slave-holder I know," he said to the runaway. "I'll have to talk to him."

The wagons drew alongside and conversation began. The slaveholder, seeing that Hyde was headed south instead of north, cracked, "Why aren't you helpin' niggers, Hyde?"

"Well, if I knew of any needin' help, I would be helpin' 'em," Hyde's replied. Then they went on their way. Hyde continued south for some distance and then turned and followed a roundabout route back to his house, concealing the runaway in his cellar that night. Nevertheless, the authorities remained suspicious and visited Hyde. To allay their suspicions, he invited them to sleep over. Little did they realize that the runaway they sought was sleeping in the cellar below them.

Hyde also hid runaways in a livery stable, in a well in which he had a platform installed where the runaways could rest while awaiting transport his cellar and in a large swamp near the town called Gaddus Lands. On one occasion, a runaway gave birth to a child at his house.[270]

This brings us up to the conclusion of our story about Hyde and Add White. The slave catchers had been absolved of any wrongdoing despite the beating of Sheriff Layton, from which he never fully recovered. The courts said it was in the marshals' legal authority to use whatever means necessary to carry out the federal warrant. In addition to the original four men who were arrested, indictments for obstructing justice were brought against Layton; Deputy Sheriff Compton; Sheriff Clark; state representative Joseph C. Brand; Judge Ichabod Corwin; Elijah Coffin of Richmond, Indiana; John S. Haukes; and Sheriff Daniel Lewis, who led the posse and made the arrest of the marshals in Lumberton.

As their friends awaited their days in court, White it is believed had been sent on the UGRR to Canada; Hyde was hiding out in the Gaddus Lands and sneaking over for dinner at Alexander Doty's. According to his daughter, Amanda, he didn't return home for nine months.[271]

An interesting sidenote, which really should be a highlight in itself, is the incident in which two fugitives from slavery were found hiding out in a room rented by *Cincinnati Daily Commercial* reporter William M. Connelly. About three weeks after breaking into Hyde's cabin, Churchill, Elliott and company broke into this room in Cincinnati. But this time, they got more than they bargained for. A scuffle followed during which one of the fugitives was shot and Elliott was stabbed in the torso. For a time, it looked like neither would survive, but Elliott pulled through—not so for the fugitive.

Connelly immediately fled to New York. More than a year passed before he was discovered and brought back to Cincinnati for trial. To the satisfaction of the city's residents, Judge Leavitt, the same judge who had absolved the marshals in the Add White rendition, let him off easy with a sentence of twenty days in jail and a fine of ten dollars. When Connelly was released in June 1858, a great celebration for his courageous deeds awaited him. The *Belmont Chronicle* described his "liberation":

> *A great torchlight procession assembled to escort him from the jail. The procession is said to have numbered three thousand persons. The* Commercial *says they were preceded by the band of the Turners's band [a local German organization], and an American flag, behind which were a couple of carriage, one of which contained Judge Stallo and Mr. Albert Lewis, and several other personal friends of Connelly. The rain poured in torrents, but it did not appear to dampen the enthusiasm of the multitude.*[272]

It seems that by 1858, the ring of fire had made its way south.

Now we return to Hyde and White. It all ended up well, for both of them and for all those indicted. The enduring pressure on all parties led Add's owner, Daniel White, to ask for a financial settlement. A sum of $950 was raised, and he signed Add's emancipation papers. Soon after, both Add and Hyde returned to Mechanicsburg, where both lived out the rest of their lives—Add serving in the war with Company E, Fifty-Fourth Massachusetts Infantry. Add and the wife he had left in Kentucky had split, and he married his second wife, Rachel, and became a familiar face in the town, driving the water wagon. Hyde married a second time, a woman thirty years his junior, and anxiously sat out the Civil War while his sons, Russell and Frank, served. One time, a fugitive, Leo L. Lloyd, whom Hyde had aided, came back to see him. Hyde recognized him immediately.

"Whatta you doin' here, nigger?"

"Mr. Hyde, I have a good job and some money. I've always wanted to repay you for saving me, so I came back to give this to you as a token of appreciation."

Lloyd said he had purchased it in Africa on a visit to see his parents. He opened the package. It was a cane with an ebony head.[273]

Incidentally, Hyde steered clear of the UGRR business after the White affair was settled, or so it was told. In all he said he aided about 513 or 517 fugitives (sources vary) during his six years working the road.[274]

William Cratty

The aforementioned William Cratty, who lived five miles east of Delaware just west of the Scioto River, is said to have aided three thousand fugitives in period spanning 1835 to 1853, with a few years off pursuing the California

Gold Rush. Judging by these alleged credentials, he deserves a place in the ring of fire. It was said, by Cratty and others, that a reward of $3,000 was offered for him in Kentucky, dead or alive.[275] Perhaps, it is apocryphal of the boast of three thousand, but he was right on the line of traffic where fugitives could go straight north to Sandusky[276] or veer east up through Alum Creek and Oberlin and then to a number of other Lake Erie ports with boats going to Canada West:

> For years and years I never opened my door at night without first taking the precaution to step back, as I drew the door open…I knew very well that the slave hunters had taken an oath to kill me….[A]t one time I had thirteen negroes in my hayloft…
>
> I once helped a runaway slave from North Carolina who stayed in my house several days. His feet, were badly frozen. He had requested his master to sell him his freedom, but his owner would not do it. Then he made up his mind to run away and managed to escape to the Mississippi River, near New Orleans. But the hounds were soon close on his track and gaining on him rapidly. Most slaveowners then kept a pack of bloodhounds with which to track the negroes. Well, it was between the alligators and the bloodhounds, and so he pitched into the river, where the dogs could not follow him. He traveled up the north shore several nights, occasionally stopping at a negro hut to get something to eat. Finally, he reached my house with his feet frozen. He stayed there several days recuperating.

In another account, Cratty told of the time he had hidden a fugitive family at his sister's house:

> In the last scrape I had…a colored man, woman and two children were hid.…As my sister was starting for church she saw two men ride up, inspect the wagon and buggy tracks until they turned in at her gate. Those two men were watching for that family of negroes, and when they saw that the wagon tracks turned in at my sister's gate they appeared to be satisfied.…I went to church and Peggy met me and told me…she was convinced that the two men had gone to get a lot of negro-hunters and would watch the house.…I immediately left, went to my sister's house and told the [family] that they must light out of there! They were a little doubtful. But I convinced them I was their true friend. The cornfield came up right to the back of the house, and I took the fugitives through this field to into my own house, about a mile distant.

Just as we were sitting down to dinner my brother. John came running along...there were about seventy-five negro hunters around our sister's house. I did not know what to do for a moment. I asked the man and woman if they were willing to be separated, and said to the woman: A man can get away, but as for you and the children, I am a little doubtful. Finally she said: If we go back, we will all go back together. That settled it!

I took them down through the meadow, about a quarter of a mile, to another meadow, dotted with new haystacks. Half a mile beyond were woods loading to the back part of my farm, where there was a dense hazel thicket. Now, said I, you stay here and I'll return about dark and take you away. I returned to my sister's and found that she and her husband refused to admit the slave hunters. This obliged them to secure a search warrant. The local squire was a member of the Presbyterian Church and he would not issue a search warrant on Sunday, so they had to wait until Monday morning...

Meantime I had taken one or two abolitionists with me, found my negroes in the hazel brush and I took them clear to the hills on this side of Delaware. I was able to do this because I knew the ins and outs of a cow path that led through the fields and woods and did not come out on the open road until the top of the hill was reached. There, we left them with an old Irishman, an abolitionist, and the next night my brother John and I took them on to Alum Creek. This was the way the business of the underground railroad was conducted![277]

THE BENEDICTS

Of the hundreds of fugitives transported by Hyde and Cratty, many of them passed through the Alum Creek Quaker Settlement. According to legend, the route there was called the Sycamore Trail because the white-barked trees that ran along the creek seemed to lead the way. It was the domain of the Benedict family. Cyrus Benedict founded it in Marengo, thirty miles north of Columbus, Ohio, in 1811. He moved there from Peru in northern New York and was followed by family members from Connecticut. At least nine members of their clan participated: Cyrus and Reuben, the patriarchs who started the involvement in the UGRR; their sons, Aaron Lancaster, Aaron, Daniel and Martin; and the third generation, Griffith, Livius and Mordecai, the son of Aaron, who began

Aaron L. Benedict House. *Courtesy Tom Calarco.*

when he was only six years old. According to Griffith, the son of Aaron L., their house was the "headquarters" of the local UGRR:[278]

> *Sometimes they were put in the cellar, but there was no cellar arranged expressly for that purpose. We kept them in the house generally, spreading beds for them on the floor. Often we had to get up and cook a meal for them in the night.*[279]

Stories about the Benedicts' involvement in the Underground Railroad begin during the 1830s. While most of the details come from the family and cousins Aaron and Aaron Lancaster Benedict, references to and accounts mentioning them from those not related to the family are numerous in the Siebert Collection.

A particularly active time was the summer of 1844. Daniel Osborn, one of the Alum Creek conductors not in the Benedict family, recorded aiding forty-five fugitives himself during a five-month period from April 14 to

126

Aaron L. Benedict. *Courtesy Ohio History Center*.

September 10. All but two from Virginia came from Kentucky. Among them were a black man who went from Ohio to Kentucky and returned with his wife, child and sister-in-law. Another was a woman who came from Canada and brought back four of her children and a grandchild from Kentucky.[280]

The passage of the Fugitive Slave Act of 1850 ushered in another period of high activity at Alum Creek. A particularly busy period occurred during the years of 1854 and 1855. This high activity corresponds to periods of high activity in others areas like Detroit and Albany and Syracuse, New York. For example, during one month during in the year 1854 or 1855, Aaron L. Benedict aided as many as sixty fugitives. In 1856, a group of thirty-three came and were distributed in the community for temporary harboring. On another occasion, he entertained twenty for dinner.[281]

One of their memorable successes was the rescue in 1839 of "Black Bill." He had run away from the Kanawha Salt Works in Virginia. It is reminiscent of the escape of Louis in Cincinnati fourteen years later and likely known of by Quaker Levi Coffin, who was involved in Louis's escape and knew those at Alum Creek. Also known as Mitchell and Anderson, Bill came to Marion, Ohio, in the fall of 1838 and worked as a butcher, barber and laborer. He was a talented fiddle, banjo player and singer and became popular at dances in the Marion social scene. But someone recognized him and informed his former master, who came to claim him. The judge said that he needed proof of ownership. The slaveholder returned home to gather witnesses, and Bill was put in a holding cell.

Shortly before the trial, Bill's wife asked those at Alum Creek for help. Nine men went to Marion, including several of the Benedicts and William Cratty. They spoke to Bill before the trial, and he said he knew all the men who had arrived in town to identify him. Realizing that there was no hope the judge would rule in his favor, their only resort was to plan an escape.

They asked a black friend of Bill's who had been trying to find a way to break Bill out of jail if he would help out. The Quakers planned to surround Bill immediately after the judge's decision and block the path of the authorities while Bill ran to a nearby field, where his black friend and two horses would be waiting.

The trial turned out to be a kind of comedy of errors. It seemed three of the witnesses had been Bill's owners—former owners, that is—and there was some confusion about who his owner at this point in time really was. The judge became puzzled; he called for adjournment. He would make his decision in the morning.

Although no witnesses appeared for Bill—and according to the laws of that time he wasn't allowed to testify on his own behalf—what had seemed like an open-and-shut case was now a bit in doubt. That night, Aaron Benedict visited Bill in jail and advised him of what he needed to do to make his escape. Bill gripped Benedict's hand: "I had prayed to the Lord, as strong as a yoke of oxen can pull, to free me from my cruel masters."

The next day, the courtroom overflowed, the horses were in place and the resistance was prepared to resist. It was time for the judge's decision. The judge cleared his throat a few times, and the courtroom became very quiet. "It appears," said the judge, "that this man has had many owners." He paused and looked around the room. "And, even you are not sure if you are really his owners, and if you can't be sure, then how in the Good Lord's name, do you expect me to be. Consequently, as I am unable to determine who is the true owner of the defendant, I have to rule in favor of Mr. Anderson."

The courtroom gasped. The sheriff said to Bill that he was free, and the courtroom erupted. Bill's alleged owner grabbed him by the neck and held a Bowie knife up against it. The sheriff said to let him go. Here's what Aaron Benedict, who was there, said happened next:

The Sheriff then called upon the by-standers to arrest him and all others that interfered with him…there was a rush made for the colored man on both sides. Then commenced…pulling, hauling, tearing of clothes…. We tried to block the way and not let them down stairs, but they soon started down taking the blockade with them, all mixed up, friend and foe. When we got to the foot of the stairs I had hold of the colored man's arm. He was struggling to free himself from the two men who had hold of him. The colored man grabbed my arm near my shoulder and held onto it as…in a vise. The slaveholder and his aids formed a ring around us flourishing knives, pistols and clubs, hallooing at the crowd, "stand back, stand back."

Women were at the upper windows screaming as we went past. We went north, I should think fifteen rods, crossing the street to the west side where there was a small building I took to be some kind of a shop. In front of this the colored man made an extra effort to free himself. He still held onto my arm. Several times men took hold of me to pull me away, but did not succeed. The would-be master threatened to shoot me. A stone was thrown at him which just grazed his face. This so exasperated him that he held the muzzle of his pistol within a few inches of my breast and...the Sheriff then ordered out the militia.

They succeeded in hauling the colored man into the building and shutting the door. There was a post and rail fence back of the building, rails were got and the door punched in. Instantly a man stood in the door swinging a bowie knife back and forth, saying, "Stand back, stand back." By this time men were there with muskets with bayonets on them. One man came running with three or four muskets, handing them to anyone who would, take them, keeping one himself. He ran up in front of the man in the door and made a thrust at him.

His brother caught his arm and turned the bayonet. It entered the door casing and was bent around like a fish-hook. I saw at once that the man was excitedly insane, and it took his brother and two other men to disarm him. The man in the door sprang back. Cyrus Benedict and Eben Daniel, of Shaw Creek, then went in. I heard lively times inside. I soon saw the fugitive and his colored friend run from the back end of the building, Goshorn, the lawyer, after them, and Cyrus Benedict after Goshorn. They ran across Main Street and down a street running east. Cyrus caught Goshorn as they ran and threw him, falling on top. Another one of the Virginians came running up and struck Cyrus a glancing blow on the side of his head with a pistol, cutting his head so it bled freely. Cyrus clinched with him and threw him; they rolled over and over several times. Cyrus' brother, William, came up and...struck the Virginian a severe blow. That put a stop to any further trouble with him. Goshorn was sitting up in the street vomiting blood. The Sheriff soon came and took them to jail. This ended the affray.[282]

Bill managed to escape with his friend and met up with Aaron Benedict. On their way to Alum Creek, they were met by Aaron's brother Martin, after which they all rode as a posse to the home of Reuben Benedict, their father—a good three or four hours' ride. He was safe now with the Virginians locked up in jail. After resting several days with the Benedicts, Bill was taken by Aaron's uncle, Aaron L. Benedict, and his brother-in-law, Griffith Levering, to the Owl Creek Friends settlement, to Oberlin and eventually to Canada.[283]

A tragic incident involved a runaway, John Green, who came to Alum Creek in 1837.[284] He had left his wife and children, and he hoped to rescue them. Aaron L. Benedict sympathized with him and gave him a job. He grew close with him and promised to help him to rescue his family. Finally, they set out in the evening in a two-horse carriage and drove to Ripley. It was early autumn and the weather amenable. They met with John Rankin, and one of the Rankin family took Green in a rowboat across river. They told him that he should return to that spot and light a fire to signal when he was ready to return. Naturally, all travel was to be done during the night, and Green set out alone on the sixty-mile journey into Kentucky.

Two weeks later, Green returned with his family. One of the Rankin boys retrieved them. While it was advisable for him and his family to move farther north, he had become attached to the community and wanted to stay longer. One night about six weeks later, while Green was away hunting, several men arrived in a wagon and abducted his wife and children. Someone spotted the wagon pulling away and blew the horn warning the settlement. Green and Aaron Benedict chased them on horseback to Delaware and attempted to get a warrant to stop them but couldn't find the sheriff. Finally, they found a police official near Bellepoint on the Scioto River, just south of Delaware. They followed the kidnappers as far as West Jefferson. The constable took them into a barroom and had a drink. He told them he could not serve the warrant.

Regrettably, it was decided that it no longer was safe for John Green in Alum Creek, and it would be foolhardy for him to try and rescue them again. He was sent along the Underground Railroad to Canada. After the Civil War, he returned and went to Kentucky, where he located his daughter, and brought her and her husband back to Ohio, where they settled in Van Wert County.

Another time, a young fugitive came with his master's prized racehorse.[285] His master followed horse racing, and he would go along on his trips to take care of the horse and race it. They had raced in Columbus, so he was familiar with the roads. His master was good to him—that is, when he was winning. When the horse got beaten, he got beaten, with a whip. Finally, he decided he had enough. His plan was to create a disguise with false whiskers.

It was made of black sheepskin that was shaped appropriately in the form of goatee on a wire that attached around his neck. The next time they raced in Ohio, he would use it to escape.

He was prepared when they went to race in Chillicothe. His plan was to win every race and, during their celebration, get his master so drunk that he would pass out. Then he would put on his master's clothes and his disguise and race away to Canada. With a horse as fast as this one, they'd never catch him. It all worked as planned, and after a short stay to tell his tale, he left Alum Creek for Canada. Later, the folks at Alum Creek received word of his arrival.

The Slave Rescuer

A much-publicized incident in 1849 involved a member of the Alum Creek settlement. Richard Dillingham was truly one of those knights in shining armor that you read about in the fairy tales. But reading his words and his story makes one wonder—how can anyone be that good?

His father, Micah, was involved with Benedicts, and Richard was a schoolteacher and passionately involved in abolitionism. He had taught in prisons and to black children. In 1847, he was among a group of Quaker abolitionists that helped forty-five black settlers in Michigan move from Cass County to Battle Creek after the infamous Kentucky Raid of 1847. In December 1848, while Richard was teaching black children in Cincinnati, one of the children's families asked him to go to Nashville, Tennessee, to bring out some of their family members who were a suffering under a cruel master.

In December 1848, he went to Nashville. He hired a free black man to drive a carriage to transport the three slaves while he rode alongside on horseback. When they reached the bridge to cross the Cumberland River, he rode ahead to pay the toll. The man smiled at him. He wasn't the toll collector. He was a law enforcement officer. "You are just the man we wanted," said Constable M.D. Maddox, "and we will make an example of you."[286]

They arrested him, and the slaves and driver, and sent them to jail. He learned that someone he knew had informed the authorities of his plan. The hostility toward him in the community was so vicious that the authorities feared that if they took out of the jail he would face an uncontrollable mob that would lynch him.

From the outset, Dillingham readily admitted his guilt and prepared himself to face the consequences. "I have no hopes of getting clear of being convicted and sentenced to the Penitentiary; but do not think that I am without comfort in my afflictions," he wrote in a letter from the jail where he spent four months before being brought to trial. "I have a clear conscience before my God, which is my greatest comfort and support through all my troubles and afflictions. The greatest affliction I have is the reflection of the sorrow and anxiety my friends will have to endure on my account."[287]

Dillingham's demeanor and honesty impressed all who met him, and the charges might have been dropped had he implicated those who had helped him arrange the escape. But he said in his letters that he knew that those he might implicate would likely face worse consequences than him, and he didn't want others to suffer on his account.

He had other opportunities to free himself. A man came and offered to pay his bail, which was set at $7,000, too much for family or friends to cover. However, when he learned that the funds were obtained through illegal means, he declined the offer. He also was offered saws and files with which to make a jailbreak, but he refused these as well. "Thou need not fear that I shall ever stoop to dishonorable means to avoid my severe impending fate," he wrote in another letter.[288]

His mother and her brother attended his trial, which took place 750 miles from Morrow County, and sat by his side. Dillingham pleaded guilty to the charges but made a plea to the jury before it decided on a verdict. "I have violated your laws," he said. "I now stand before you, to my sorrow and regret, as a criminal. But I was prompted to it by feelings of humanity. It has been suspected, as I was informed, that I am leagued with a fraternity who are combined for the purpose of committing such offences as the one with which I am charged. But gentlemen, the impression is false. I alone am guilty—I alone committed the offence—and I alone must suffer the penalty."[289]

He then begged forgiveness and leniency considering the age and poor health of his parents and the likelihood that his imprisonment would severely harm them.[290] At the conclusion of his plea, it is said that most of those in the jury were actually weeping. They retired and quickly reached their verdict: three years in the penitentiary, the shortest allowable sentence.

The warden of the penitentiary, John McIntosh, thought the sentence too light and at first was prejudiced against him. However, Dillingham's steadfast acceptance of his situation and innate kindness won his favor. As a result, after nine months spent breaking stones in hard labor, McIntosh moved Dillingham to the prison hospital to care for sick inmates. Dillingham seemed to have found his vocation. He worked out so well that the warden moved him into more comfortable quarters where he had more light to read, and with the approval of the warden, he was also given medical books to study. "I enjoy the comforts of a good fire and a warm room, and am allowed to sit up evenings and read, which I prize as a great privilege."[291]

Dillingham, who was engaged to be married when he was arrested, had released his fiancée from her vows, and she promised to wait for him. But a cholera epidemic broke out at the prison. He was working around the clock when one morning he became ill. By the afternoon, his mortal shell had succumbed to the disease. His life surely exemplified these words he wrote in prison:

> *The nearer I live to the commandment Love thy neighbor as thyself, the more enjoyment I have of this life. None can know the enjoyments that flow from feelings of goodwill toward our fellow human beings, both friends and enemies, but those who feel and cultivate them.*[292]

McIntosh and another prison official were moved to write sincere letters of regret and sympathy to Dillingham's family, yet they buried him in an unmarked grave.

Dillingham was only one among hundreds of good country people who composed this ring of abolitionist fire. There were victories and there were losses. It was a preview of the Civil War.

Chapter 12

THE REAL MEANING OF THE UNDERGROUND RAILROAD

As the Civil War drew near, tensions progressively heightened between the North and the South. The election of Lincoln, a moderate Republican who opposed slavery on moral grounds, was about to push the South over the edge. It no longer had the decided political advantage in the federal government that it had throughout most of the nation's history and which helped the region maintain the system of slavery.[293] Things were shifting, although the South hadn't completely lost its grip, as the Dred Scott decision illustrated. But those who opposed slavery were growing in the North, as was the violence that resulted from the clash between the state and federal authorities. Nothing better illustrated this than the incident on September 20, 1860, at Iberia College, which was about ten miles north of the Alum Creek settlement.

Iberia College was opened in 1854, the offspring of John Rankin's Free Presbyterian Synod, which was founded on antislavery principles in 1840 and which by the Civil War had seventy-two member churches.[294] John Robb, who moved there some years later, heard a lot about it:

> When I lived in Iberia I heard a good I deal about the times before the war. An old gentleman, Robert McClarren told me more than once about what he called the "Nigger Scrape" he and others got into when George Gordon was President of the College.
>
> Two colored men were kept and employed by some of the farmers near Iberia. These men were...fugitives from Kentucky. Their owners learned of

their whereabouts, and came with United States officers to take them. The people of Iberia...rose up en mass to resist the officers....The would-be captors were captured and tied, wattles were cut from the beech trees, and put into the hands of the negro slaves, with the injunction to lay on.[295]

Archy Brownlee not only was a longtime resident of Iberia but also had been a confirmed abolitionist for twenty years and a regular participant in the UGRR. He was living there when everything took place:

The last slave catcher that ever came on the track was in the fall of 1860 when six men from the South got off the train, two miles south of Iberia station....Suspicion was excited that they were slave catchers....It was well known that three fugitives, the names of Martin brothers were living at three adjoining farmhouses about 2 miles west of the railroad in the direction the men were going so that there was a general rush of citizens and students. Iberia College at that time was in the care of the free Presbyterian Church with about 1/3 of the students colored....At house Nos. 2 and 3 they nipped their man as two colored students passed into the yard of house No. 2. They met the two slave catchers coming out of the house....The negroes [students] *supposing the whites might be members of the family bade them good coming. One of the men stepped up and laid his hand on the shoulder* [one of the students] *and said is this your boy when both parties drew their pistols so near the same time that* [the student] *Asberry supposed that he had fired twice, but he was mistaken for the firing was done by the other party...the* [other black student, Douglass] *found that his weapon had miss fired as none of the loads had been discharged. Asberry was shot through the right hand....The second shot cut through the left sleeve of his coat...near the skin as to leave a blue spot.* [Asberry himself told Brownlee]. *Douglass was so near his man that he could only use his gun as a bludgeon by which he brought his man to the ground. At this point the two white men ran perhaps caused by seeing other parties coming to the field of strife. At any rate the men were pursued and quickly captured, stripped and tied to a tree and whipped on back with beech rods by the negroes.*

There were about 25 or 30 persons present but none of them took an active part in the whipping except the negroes. Rev. Gordon talked to them by telling them they engaged in a bad cause....At the first setting of the U.S. Supreme Court in Cleveland about 20 of our boys were indicted for a breach of the fugitive slave law. Rev. George Gordon was the only person that was convicted.[296]

It had come to this—black college students beating federal marshals and getting off. Only an innocent man received punishment. Reverend George Gordon, a Presbyterian minister from Pennsylvania who joined the synod to become its first college president, wrote of his defiance at his sentencing of eleven months in jail:

> *I have no favors to crave, no mercy to implore. I stand erect in conscious integrity and manhood. My household has ever been a home for the fleeing fugitive and shall be so still. If my dwelling be reduced to a cabin, he shall be welcome to a corner. All the devils in hell and the slave catchers out of hell shall not close my door against him.* [297]

The trial of Gordon had been delayed on the advice of the court in consideration of the recent election of Lincoln. As a consequence, Gordon went to Canada. It was after the conflagration began at Fort Sumter that he returned to answer to the charges of obstructing the arrest by the marshals under the FSL. With Lincoln in office, he never expected to be convicted, especially in light of the fact that while he witnessed the beatings, he advised the students to desist.[298] But one must remember that at the time, Lincoln was more concerned with saving the Union than ending slavery, as he wrote to Horace Greeley in 1862: "My paramount object in this struggle is to save the Union, and is not either to save or to destroy slavery. If I could save the Union without freeing any slave I would do it."

In jail, Gordon found his conditions almost intolerable. An inmate stole some of Gordon's clothing and wore it to make his escape. For this, Gordon was blamed and put in a basement with only a gaslight to reckon his waking hours. His health sank, and his friends petitioned Lincoln for a pardon, even though Gordon begged off because it would imply guilt. Finally, he gave in, and on April 4, 1862, after five months in jail, he was released. However, he never recovered his health and died five years later.[299]

So many Purple Hearts could have been awarded to these "seekers of alternative veteranhood," as one contemporary historian has mocked them. Certainly, however, there are more than enough documented incidents that show without a shred of doubt the battles that took place because of aid given to fugitive slaves in Ohio. And the corroborative testimonies of men who hadn't seen each other in decades but told similar or exact stories should vanquish any doubts of their veracity. But then there is the question of exaggeration, of doubts about the extent of the UGRR, about who was in charge or if there even was enough of an organization to say that

Reverend George
Gordon's grave site.
Courtesy Tom Calarco.

someone was in charge. This book has already supplied much material to counter that. Nevertheless, it has become necessary to show that the truth is closer to the actual legend of an organized effort of abolitionists north of the Mason-Dixon line and that its legend is the real core of its meaning to American history.

Another of the legendary accounts that has been called into question and that is seldom referenced by "serious" mainstream historians is William M. Cockrum's 1915 book, *History of the Underground Railroad: As It Was Conducted by the Antislavery League.* It's a folksy narrative, using terms with a racist tinge like "darkies" that also are commonly used by the Siebert's respondents writing in the 1890s. It's written in a playful tone, with a series of vignettes illustrating how cowboy abolitionists in Indiana continually outwitted slave catchers. But it also made some amazing claims, some of which are probably exaggerated but others that have never been proven or conclusively denied.

Cockrum described the Anti-Slavery League (ASL) as an organization formed in 1852 by abolitionists in the East that sent agents into the South to aid fugitives in their escape to freedom. Its agents included well-educated young and middle-aged men who posed as fishermen, teachers, mapmakers, mineralogists, clock tinkers and book peddlers. They were organized and supplied. Some of the procedures they followed included living in fish shacks along the Ohio River. There they could more easily help fugitives

Left: William L. Cockrum *Right*: John Hansen of Hanover.

crossing over. They were especially active at night and used turpentine balls to signal boatman along the river to pick up fugitives. Also, to throw off as bloodhounds, they spread red pepper along the pathways. They sometimes carried Sharps rifles hidden under long coats slung under their arms and sometimes blackened their faces to disguise their identities.

The leader of the league in Indiana was John Hansen, which was an alias. He later revealed his true identity, John Hanover, in a letter to Cockrum after the Civil War, when he was working for the Freedmen's Bureau. In it, he alleged that the league aided four thousand fugitives annually at the Ohio River crossing. While this might be an exaggeration, numbers reported in places like Detroit indicate that it could have approached this in its peak years. Remember, the ASL of Cockrum's book operated during this period and was situated along the entire one-thousand-mile stretch of the Ohio River.[300] There may be more truth to the ASL than many currently believe.

In 1855, Matt Peters, a homeless twelve-year-old boy, met Henry Roberts, an enterprising twenty-five-year-old from Cortsville, Ohio, near the Green Plain Meeting of UGRR involvement. They were in New Orleans:

> *I was a street gamin, wrote Peters, without home, family or friends, my mother and sisters had been carried off by an epidemic, and shortly after*

my father died. While loitering about the levee near the foot of Canal Street,
New Orleans, I noticed a passing dray which was followed by a man.

The wagon passed him. A short while later, the boy saw that it had stopped next to a large boat docked along the canal. It had been unloaded, and the man looked like he was paying the driver, who then pulled away. The man looked around and saw the boy approaching. He asked the boy if he would watch his cargo with boxes of oranges and bananas, some young magnolia trees and other gardening materials. He was gone for only a few minutes and gave the boy a little something. When he started to load the boat, the boy gladly pitched in. As they were loading, the man, sensing the desperation of the boy, asked more about him. Gradually, Peters began to reveal his sorrowful tale.

His father had died, and his father's friend found an apprenticeship for him with a German tailor. The man would beat him when he didn't sew properly or failed to carry out other errands properly. So, he decided to run away and live in the streets. Then and there, Roberts decided to adopt him. He told him he was from Ohio and had a mother who would take care of him; they would send him to school and teach him a trade. And so you would think that this tale had a happy ending. But there is much more.

Going up the Mississippi on the big boat called the *Gladenel*, a lot of unusual things happened. It seemed that it kept making stops during the night in out-of-the-way places where there was only forested areas. This is how Peters described it:

> *Here the negro deck-hands would throw out the gang-plank and hurry ashore to bring wood aboard. I noticed two or three white men at the dreary landings. My friend, the stranger, would always go ashore and after a hasty greeting engage in animated conversation with them until the whistle sounded, and he would part with them as hastily as he had gone. Not only did this occur at every one of the wood-landings we touched, but whenever the boat hauled up at a city there were always those who would rush aboard to see him or else he would hasten ashore to meet them.*

Finally, after a journey that took them up the Mississippi to the Ohio River, stopping in Louisville, they disembarked at their destination, Cincinnati, a journey of about one thousand miles. They took the train to Selma and then walked through the fields in the middle of the night to Roberts's homestead. They were greeted by his gray-haired mother and even older aunt who was bent and walked with a cane. Shortly after their arrival, Roberts was called to go on a trip to Canada. Several days after Roberts returned, he was seized by a severe illness and suddenly died.

It was then that his mother told him the real story behind his trips to the South and Canada. He had quit his blacksmith business and was devoting his life to the liberation of the slaves. He felt the need to go among the slaves and deliver the gospel of freedom. Those friends in the South, she said, were agents of the UGRR. These individuals would go into the South during the winter and work as mechanics, carpenters, blacksmiths or overseers on the plantations during the planting and harvesting seasons. The stops along the river would ostensibly be to load wood for fuel but also to load fugitives aided by the suppliers of the wood, who were Northerners who had gone south and worked as contractors for the boat trade. Roberts's mother told Peters that he had brought eighteen fugitives to freedom during his last trip.[301]

Far-fetched as some may believe it to be, another story adds corroboration. It deals with a former Oberlin student, Charles Brown, a free black man originally from South Carolina but who wandered into Cincinnati, where he became acquainted with the abolitionists. It led to Oberlin, where he acquired the minimal education that he received, and then to New Orleans. It seems he and three other black men attempted to rob a bank in New Orleans, during which several bank employees died—at least one murdered and the others dying in the fire that nearly burned the bank to the ground. While awaiting his execution, Brown was interviewed for a book of confessions by a local journalist:

> *I know that my career in life is nearly run—that in a few more hours I must stand in the presence of my God, to render up an account of my stewardship. The sentence of the law has been passed upon me, and I know there is no power on earth that will interpose to save me from the doom under which I labor. I go to meet my God. Before I enter the bar of that tribunal, before whom all must stand, I, in compliance with what I esteem a duty to my fellow-men, make this, my solemn confession of the acts of my life.*
>
> *During the time I was at Oberlin, a Convention of the Anti-Slavery Society of Ohio was held there....I agreed to embark in the cause and assist in carrying out their schemes as also to incorporate myself as a member of the society. I have continued in the employ of the society up to the present time.*
>
> *There are auxiliary societies in nearly every town of any note on the Ohio River...and in most of the principal towns in the interior. The largest*

portion of the members…are willing to contribute money to aid in the relief of slaves…but are seldom engaged in the active duties of running off or secreting them. I believe the whole number now enrolled in the Ohio State Society is about 18,000.[302]

Every society has a President, Secretary, Treasurer and other active officers and members, to whom the secret operations of the society alone are entrusted. The agents are employed by the State society. They have employed in the State of Virginia, South Carolina, Kentucky and the South and South-western states about one hundred and fifty agents. Some of them however are under pay from the Boston and other eastern Antislavery societies. These agents are either stationary or travelling as circumstances may require.

There is an entire reciprocity and a constant correspondence kept up between the Ohio State Anti-slavery Society and the Anti-slavery society of Boston, New York and other eastern towns. The agent of any society may send a slave to the care of any other and he will be received and treated in the same manner as if he was sent to the society to which the Agent belongs. Every agent knows the active members of all the societies and when and how to direct the runaway slave where to go and to whom to apply for assistance when he arrives at the place of destination.

The agents are paid various sums, from 20 to $50 per month by the society which sends them out, according to their zeal and success and the danger and risk they encounter. Then their pay and provision for enabling poor runaway slaves to get off is made in this manner: there is a small contribution levied on every member of the society. This goes into the Treasury. It is the duty of the Agent to prevail on slaves to run away from their masters, and when he finds one willing to go he is at liberty to advise him to steal and take with him any of his master's money or property which he can obtain the possession of. This is not regarded as stealing in a criminal sense, for the servant, who is regarded as free by the law of nature, having assisted the master in accumulating the money or property has as much right…to a portion of it.…The slave will be sent to any place he may desire but if he has no particular place…the agent may send him to any town where there is a society. He is directed…to go directly to a certain place and enquire for certain persons, generally blacks; to these he communicates…that he is a runaway slave and they inform the officers of the society, [who make] *arrangements made for sending him off or secreting him. If he has no money a draft is made on the Treasury for a sufficient sum to defray expenses. When the runaway has money it* *is usually suggested…that he…pay into the Treasury something…for the assistance…and something to help off those unable to help themselves. The amount is left to himself. Besides this, he will give the agent, who helps him off, something. This the Agent has the right to keep over and above the pay he draws from the society.*

Every member of the society knows that slaves are induced to run away, but very few know who is the agent that induced or helped them off. When a runaway arrives at a place, a great many members may know that there is a runaway in town, but generally it is kept as quiet as possible. The sending him away, or secreting him, is usually entrusted to only two or three, and generally no one but themselves knows where he has been sent to. If the slave has no place he can secrete himself, in the interior of the states, he is usually sent directly to Canada.[303]

Madison Henderson, the leader of the gang that held up the bank, had this to say about Brown during his last interview and confession:

I first saw Charles Brown, the man who has been condemned with me, in New Orleans some weeks before Gen. Jackson visited there to lay the corner stone of the monument.[304] *Brown had been on the St. Louis steamboat as a barber, but had left her. He had some way heard of me and came one day to the store. He talked to me some time, but generally kept a good way off; and as I did not know anything about him, I was rather shy of him. During our conversations at subsequent periods he informed me that his principal business was to run away slaves, and that he was in the employ of the Abolition Society; told me how he accomplished it, and said that when the steamboat Captains would not take them on board for him, he got some white man to go on board and engage their passage. He wanted me to run off [some] and from his proposing this to me, as I knew a good deal about the coaxing of negroes off, I didn't believe much in him. After some time I tried him another way, my object was to ascertain if he was a black leg. One day when he was talking to me, I asked him for the loan of $100 until the next day. This he readily lent me, and the next day I returned him a $50 bill he had lent me, and $50 in silver. He wished me to keep it longer but I declined. He told me I could have 4 or $500 whenever I wanted it.*[305]

If these three separate, unrelated but corroborative stories about the organization of the UGRR are true, then we are looking at a UGRR that is much closer to the one of lore and legend worthy of singing songs about.

But before we leave this legend, there is one more important legacy of the Underground Railroad that is overlooked, one integral to keeping our nation the land of the free and the home of the brave. It is the right to speak freely and to oppose with words and feelings all that is unjust, cruel, immoral and degrading to our fellow human beings.

It is the legacy of civil disobedience. It is a legacy that was best expressed by Henry David Thoreau. Few realize that before he was locked up in jail for nonpayment of his taxes, his mother and sisters were the leaders of the Concord Female Anti-Slavery Society and warmly patronized by William Lloyd Garrison. Thoreau also escorted at least one fugitive to the train in Concord, which was bound for Canada, and it is believed that he escorted others.[306] Who can say it better than this? Who can articulate better the idea behind obeying the higher law, as the abolitionists referred to it—the cornerstone of the belief system of the Underground Railroad:

> *I think that we should be men first, and subjects afterward. It is not desirable to cultivate a respect for the law, so much as for the right. The only obligation which I have a right to assume, is to do at any time what I think right....Law never made men a whit more just; and, by means of their respect for it, even the well-disposed are daily made the agents of injustice. A common and natural result of an undue respect for law is, that you may see a file of soldiers, colonel, captain, corporal, privates, powder-monkeys and all, marching in admirable order over hill and dale to the wars, against their wills, aye, against their common sense and consciences, which makes it very steep marching indeed, and produces a palpitation of the heart. They have no doubt that it is a damnable business in which they are concerned.[307]*

Before concluding this examination of the Underground Railroad, with all this sorrow and death and sacrifice that has come before you, dear reader, it's time for a feel-good story.

Anna Millie Wright was a slave in Tennessee when she was fifteen years old. She was sold on the auction block with her infant daughter, who was, in turn, sold away from her. Anna was purchased by Dover, Tennessee slaveholder William Brandon. As his slave, she had seven more children, by whose paternity it is not known. But each of her children was sold away. Finally, she ran away, crossing the Ohio by Ripley. Through the UGRR, she reached Xenia, where she met and married Jackson Wright and blended into the community. In 1870, they moved to Findlay, and in 1882, her husband died. For years, she had been advertising through the networks of the black churches for information about any of her children. In 1892, a chance remark was made by a man visiting from West Virginia about a woman in his town of Clarksburg who had been inquiring if anyone knew of relatives who had been sold in Dover, Tennessee. On a hunch, Wright wrote to the pastor of the black church there. There was no answer, so she tried again, asking if anyone knew about the Brandon family. The letter was read at the church service, and the woman who had been inquiring about Dover, Tennessee, was there and burst out with an exclamation. The next day, she wrote to Wright all the details of her life and her brothers and sisters that she knew about, and all the details fit. Finally, after parting at the slave block so many years before, they rejoiced in their reunion.[308]

That is the legend of the Underground Railroad—the legend we should revere, the legend that puts truth and goodness above all, the empathy for suffering that is pure love. It is to them we should build monuments, the real heroes of American history, the ones who battled for suffering humanity, some even making the ultimate sacrifice. It's a good legend. And even if it were untrue—which it isn't—it's such a wonderful legend. May it live forever in the annals of American history.

Appendix

THE FUGITIVE SLAVE LAWS

T he first law concerning fugitive slaves was passed in 1793. It was a
national law and the first of many to follow, which were state laws,
culminating in the infamous Fugitive Slave Act of 1850. The former
imposed a fine of $500—equal to $7,500 today—and up to one year in prison
for every slave aided by those convicted. Testimony of a slave owner or his
representative before any legally appointed judge was enough to commit the
alleged fugitive to slavery. However, because of the travel and time needed
to apprehend slaves, slave owners became dependent on slave catchers. This
facilitated slave catchers in the kidnapping of free blacks and selling them
into slavery, a practice that was common already before its passage. Among
its provisions was the suspension of the alleged fugitive slave's right to a jury
trial or to testify on his or her own behalf.

In Ohio, a state fugitive slave law was passed in 1839 at the request of
the State of Kentucky, which is evidence of the high level of Underground
Railroad activity in the state. This request, in part, stated:

> [T]he injuries sustained by the citizens of Kentucky, inhabiting the counties
> bordering on the Ohio river, adjacent to this State, by the loss of their
> slaves, has ceased to be confined to a small number of persons. Facts,
> within the personal knowledge of the representatives of those counties,
> and communicated to the legislature in numerous memorials of the people,
> leave no doubt that losses are felt to an alarming extent, threatening, in the
> absence of a more efficient legislation.[309]

But on March 1, 1842, the Prigg decision of the Supreme Court decreed that states had no right to interfere with the recovery of slaves by their owners. In effect, it overruled the Ohio law and all other state laws that aided the reclamation of fugitive slaves, stating that such reclamations could be only made through the use of federal authorities. As a result, northern states made it even more cumbersome for federal officials by passing personal liberty laws that forbade the use of state officers and jails in cases involving fugitive slaves.

THE FUGITIVE SLAVE ACT OF 1850

The 1850 national law circumvented the personal liberty laws and gave total authority for the handling of fugitive slave cases to federal jurisdiction, circumventing state laws that had been established to protect the rights of the alleged fugitive. It included some of the same provisions as the earlier act and increased the fine for its violation to $1,000—equal to $24,000 today—and six months in prison for each fugitive slave assisted. All that was required for the conviction of alleged fugitive slaves was their identification by two witnesses under oath that the individual was a fugitive from slavery.

A key provision was the addition of the appointment of individuals to be appointed as special judges to adjudicate fugitive slave cases. It also established a system in which individuals were appointed to act as judges to hear cases involving the law. The judges' decisions were prejudiced by a stipulation that paid them $10 for every fugitive slave convicted and $5 for those set free. Adding force was a $1,000 fine imposed on federal marshals who failed to follow an order arrest a fugitive slave. These marshals also were liable for the value of any slave who escaped from them. Perhaps the most noxious clause of the new law was that it required citizens to assist in the rendition of a fugitive slave or face the same penalties as one who aided them. As many protested, this turned every citizen in the North into a slave catcher.

In retaliation, additional personal liberty laws were passed by a number of northern states. In some, the identity of the person claimed needed to be proven by two witnesses. If not, the alleged fugitive slave was allowed the right to a writ of habeas corpus, which gave them the opportunity to a trial by jury. The right to a public defender was also granted, and penalties were levied for false testimony. In Ohio, where the personal liberty laws were not enacted except for one year in 1857, after which it was repealed, there were many in the legal profession opposed to slavery, among them the fervent abolitionist (and senator and governor of the state during the 1850s) Salmon Chase, as well as many law enforcement officers, and this was a big help to the abolitionists. This set up the tension among state, local and federal authorities that is vividly seen in the Addison White incident.

NOTES

Introduction

1. *Freedom Seekers: Ohio and the Underground Railroad* (Columbus, OH: Friends of Freedom Society Press, 2004); Beverly J. Gray, African-American Experience in Southern Ohio, www.angelfire.com/oh/chillicothe/index.html; Henry Burke, *Washington County Underground Railroad* (Charleston, SC: Arcadia Publishing, 2004), as well as numerous articles; Cheryl Janifer LaRoche, *Free Black Communities and the Underground Railroad* (Champaign: University of Illinois Press, 2014); Karen S. Campbell, ed., *Anti-Slavery & the Underground Railroad—Taking a Risk for Freedom: Report of the Research Committee* (N.p.: Mary L. Cook Public Library, 2007); Wayne L. Snider, *All in the Same Spaceship* (New York: Vantage Press, 1974); *People, Places and Voices: Abolition and the Underground Railroad in Fayette County* (Washington Court House, OH: Washington High School, 2001); *Underground Railroad in Highland County*, Highland County Research Committee, 2016, available on DVD.

Chapter 1

2. Ralph M. Watts, "History of the Underground Railroad in Mechanicsburg," *Ohio History* 43, no. 3 (July 1934): 234–40; Benjamin F. Prince, "The Rescue Case of 1857," *Ohio History* 16, no. 3 (July 1907): 293–97.

3. *Urbana Citizen and Gazette*, "More of the Slavecatchers," May 29, 1857.

4. Amanda Shepherd to Wilbur Siebert, July 7, 1895, Wilbur Siebert Collection; *Urbana Citizen and Gazette*, "The Fugitive Slave Case," June 12, 1857; "The Rescue Case," June 19, August 14, 1857; *New York Tribune*, "The Man Hunt," June 15, 1857.

5. Amanda Shepherd to Wilbur Siebert, July 7, 1895, Wilbur Siebert Collection; *Urbana Citizen and Gazette*, "The Fugitive Slave Case," June 12, 1857; "Slavecatchers Baffled," May 22, 1857; "The Rescue Case," June 19, August 14, 1857; *New York Tribune*, "The Man Hunt," June 15, 1857.

6. Shepherd to Siebert, July 7, 1895.

7. Prince, "Rescue Case of 1857," 295.

8. Watts, "History of the Underground Railroad in Mechanicsburg," 242–43; *Urbana Citizen and Gazette*, "The Rescue Case," August 7, 1857.

9. A legal document that requires an arresting officer to show proper cause for his actions to a judge.

10. Their bill showed that thirty orders of liquor had been ordered by the slave catchers, and as some were getting drunk, Churchill actually instructed them to refrain from any further drinking.

11. Taken from testimony, *Urbana Citizen and Gazette*, "The Rescue Case," June 19, 1857; *Cincinnati Enquirer*, "The Habeas Corpus of United States Marshals," June 12, 1857.

12. *Urbana Citizen and Gazette*, "The Rescue Case," June 19, 1857; *Cincinnati Enquirer*, "The Habeas Corpus of United States Marshals," June 12, 1857.

13. Prince, "Rescue Case of 1857," 299.

14. *Urbana Citizen and Gazette*, Judge Leavitt's opinion, July 17, 1857.

15. *Anti-Slavery Bugle*, "The Habeas Corpus Case in Cincinnati," June 20, 1857.

Chapter 2

16. Lorenzo Dow Turner, *Anti-Slavery Sentiment in American Literature Prior to 1865* (Port Washington, NY: Kennikat Press, 1966), 26.

17. Wilbur H. Siebert, *The Underground Railroad: From Slavery to Freedom* (New York: Macmillan, 1898), 33.

18. Lydia Maria Child, *Isaac T. Hopper: A True Life* (Boston: John P. Jewett and Company, 1853).

19. This is about $7,500 in today's currency, according to the Inflation Calculator, https://westegg.com/inflation.

20. Carol Wilson, *Freedom at Risk: The Kidnapping of Free Blacks in America, 1780–1865* (Lexington: University Press of Kentucky, 1994), 90.

21. Ibid., 25.

22. Jon Musgrave, "Slaves, Salt, Sex, and Mr. Crenshaw," 2005, IllinoisHistory.com.

23. Freedom on the Move, freedomonthemove.org.

24. Theodore Weld, *American Slavery as It Is* (New York: American Anti-Slavery Society, 1839), 20.

25. Henry Brown, *Narrative of the Life of Henry Box Brown* (Manchester, UK: Lee and Glynn, 1851), 47.

26. Robert C. Smedley, *History of the Underground Railroad in Chester and Neighboring Counties of Pennsylvania* (Lancaster, PA: The Journal, 1883), 27–28.

27. Henry Wilson, *History of the Rise and Fall of the Slave Power in America*, vol. 2 (Boston: James R. Osgood and Company, 1874), 63.

28. *(New York City) Emancipator*, "Story from S.C.," December 28, 1837.

29. Alice Dana Adams, *The Neglected Period of Anti-Slavery in America, 1808–1831* (Cambridge, MA: Radcliffe College, 1908), 117–18.

30. Levi Coffin, *Reminiscences of Levi Coffin* (Cincinnati, OH: Robert Clarke & Company, 1880), 20–23, 74–76; Addison Coffin, *Life and Travels of Addison Coffin* (Cleveland, OH, 1897), 19.

31. Joshua Coffin, *An Account of Some of the Principal Slave Insurrections…* (New York: American Anti-Slavery Society, 1860), 32.

32. Herbert Aptheker, *American Negro Slave Revolts* (New York: Columbia University Press, 1943), 313–15; Jeffrey Ruggles, *The Unboxing of Henry Brown* (Richmond: Library of Virginia, 2003), 8; Brown, *Narrative of the Life of Henry Box Brown*, 19; Harriet Jacobs, *Incidents in the Life of a Slave Girl* (Boston, 1861), 97–103.

33. Archibald A. Grimke, *The Abolitionist* (New York: Funk & Wagnalls, 1891), 126–30; James Oliver Horton and Lois E. Horton, *In Hope of Liberty* (New York: Oxford University Press, 1997), 199.

34. Owen W. Muelder, *Theodore Dwight Weld and the American Anti-Slavery Society* (Jefferson, NC: McFarland and Company, 2011).

35. The increase in the commissioner's fee if the accused were found guilty was five dollars or seventy-five dollars per individual in today's money.

36. Don Papson and Tom Calarco, *Secret Lives of the Underground Railroad in New York City* (Jefferson, NC: McFarland and Company Inc., 2015), 107–8.

37. Ibid.

38. Ibid., 254.

39. David Cecelski, "The Shores of Freedom: The Maritime Underground Railroad in North Carolina, 1800–1861," *North Carolina Historical Review* 1, no. 2 (April 1994): 174–205.

40. Siebert, *Underground Railroad*, 146; Arch Merrill, *The Underground, Freedom's Road and Other Upstate Tales* (New York: American Book–Stratford Press, 1963), 75.

41. Stanley Harrold, *Subversives: Antislavery Community in Washington, D.C.* (Baton Rouge: Louisiana State University Press, 2003), 64–93.

42. Charles E. Barnes, "Battle Creek as a Station on the Underground Railway," *Michigan Historical Pioneer and Historical Collections* 38 (1912): 280, 283; N. Matson, *Reminiscences of Bureau County* (Princeton, IL, 1872), 364–70; Roderick Frary to Wilbur Siebert, August 3, 1896, Wilbur Siebert Collection.

43. Tom Calarco, *Places of the Underground Railroad* (Santa Barbara, CA: Greenwood Press, 2011), 341–45.

44. M.H. Peters, "An Abolitionist: A True Story of Life in Ante-Bellum Days," *Home and Country*, July 1893, 1,222–31.

Chapter 3

45. Including the following: What in your knowledge was the route of the Underground Road (names and locations of "stations" and "station keepers")? Period of activity of the "Road"? Method of operation of the "Road," with system of communication among the members? Memorable incidents (with dates, names of places and persons, as far as possible)? History of your own connection with the Underground cause? Names and present addresses of any persons able to contribute other information on the subject? Short biographical sketch of yourself?

46. Siebert, *Underground Railroad*, xxiii.

47. Larry Gara, "The Underground Railroad: A Reevaluation," *Ohio Historical Quarterly* 69 (July 1960): 217–30. Gara elaborated on these conclusions in his book published the following year.

48. Papson and Calarco, *Secret Lives of the Underground Railroad*, 107–8.

49. The number of "negroes" in Canada West, Lower Canada and Canada East, today Ontario and Quebec, was 13,566, according to *The Blacks in Canada* (New Haven, CT: Yale University Press, 1971), 486.

50. Ibid., 487, n.8.

51. Larry Gara, *Liberty Line* (Lexington: University of Kentucky Press, 1961), 43.

52. Ibid., 11–12.

53. David Blight, *Race and Reunion: The Civil War in American Memory* (Cambridge, MA: Belknap Press of Harvard University Press, 2001), 230–31, 233.

54. That number was much in the majority when Garrison started his abolitionist crusade, and while it gradually diminished, it probably was not until Lincoln was elected that antislavery became the majority view in the North.

55. Ethan Kytle and Carl Gessert, "Myth, Reality, and the Underground Railroad," *New York Times*, Opinion Pages, February 27, 2015.

56. Ibid.

57. Blight, *Race and Reunion*, 231.

58. Ibid., 233.

59. *Urbana Citizen and Gazette*, "Fugitive Slave Case."

Chapter 4

60. Nikki Taylor, *Frontiers of Freedom* (Athens: Ohio University Press, 2005), 51, n.3–7.

61. Keith Griffler, *Front Line of Freedom* (Lexington: University Press of Kentucky, 2004), 27–28.

62. *(Lebanon, OH) Western Star*, August 29, 1829; Griffler, *Front Line of Freedom*, 32–33.

63. Nelson W. Evans, *A History of Scioto County, Ohio* (Portsmouth, OH: Nelson W. Evans, 1903), 613.

64. Henry Howe, *Historical Collections of Ohio*, vol. 2 (Cincinnati, OH, 1900), 242; Carter G. Woodson, "Transplanting Free Negroes to Ohio, 1815–1858," *Journal of Negro History* 3 (January 1916): 308–9.

65. Daniel Ryan, *History of Ohio: The Rise and Progress of an American State*, vol. 4 (New York: Century History Company, 1912), 119.

66. *History of Brown County, Ohio* (Chicago: Beers and Company, 1883), 592.

67. See Paula Kitty Wright, *Gist's Promised Land* (Seaman, OH: Sugar Tree Ridge Publishing, 2013).

68. Isaac Beck to Wilbur Siebert, December 26, 1892, Wilbur Siebert Collection.

69. Gabe N. Johnson to Wilbur Siebert, November 1894, Wilbur Siebert Collection; interview with Gabe N. Johnson, September 30, 1894, Wilbur Siebert Collection.

70. Levi Coffin did not come to Cincinnati until 1848, but the UGRR was already a going concern. Coffin refined it with a more organized approach and provided better leadership.

71. Johnson's dates are confusing because it's not clear if he first visited Ironton in 1849, when he says there only fifteen houses there, or actually was living there for a period. That he says he worked in Cincinnati until 1855 suggests he wasn't permanently living in Ironton until 1855.

72. In 1827, a Mr. Ward of Pittsylvania County, Virginia, at his death, emancipated his seventy slaves, who were relocated with help from locals to Lawrence County, Ohio, according to *Ohio State Journal*, "Blacks and Mulattos," May 3, 1827; Cheryl Janifer LaRoche, "On the Edge of Freedom," diss., 2004, 289.

73. Interview with Catherine Cummings, December 23, 1893, Wilbur Siebert Collection; LaRoche, "On the Edge of Freedom," 290; Wilbur Siebert, *Mysteries of the Underground Railroad* (Columbus, OH: Long's College Book Company, 1951), 94–95; 98–99; Lawrence County Register, lawrencecountyohio.com.

74. LaRoche, "On the Edge of Freedom," 293; Lawrence County Register.

75. Howe, *Historical Collections of Ohio*, 2:62.

76. This has been disputed by the Thomas Jefferson Foundation, which directed a study of the matter in 2000 and concluded that there was no persuasive evidence that he was Jefferson's son.

77. Gray, African-American Experience.

78. Land grants made available to veterans of the Revolutionary War and their families.

79. Interview with Wilson Hawk, June 8, 1895, Wilbur Siebert Collection.

80. *Colored American*, "Colored Inhabitants of Ohio," October 31, 1840.

81. According to the research of Beverly J. Gray.

82. Lewis Woodson to Samuel E. Cornish, *Colored American*, February 7, 1838.

83. Henry Cheatam of North Carolina was elected at the same time but actually took office before Langston because of improprieties that occurred during the election process in Virginia.

84. John Mercer Langston, *From the Plantation to the National Capitol* (Hartford, CT: American Publishing Company, 1894), 12.

85. This author could not verify if he was the son of Thomas C. Woodson, whose son by that name died from a beating by a proslavery mob in 1853, according to oral tradition.

86. Wendell P. Dabney, *Cincinnati's Colored Citizens* (Cincinnati, OH: Wendell P. Dabney Publishing Company, 1926), 374.

87. Langston, *From the Plantation to the National Capitol*, 102.

88. Ibid., 21.

Chapter 5

89. Paul Goodman, *Of One Blood: Abolition and the Origin of Racial Equality* (Berkeley: University of California, 1998), 71.

90. Reverend R.C. Galbraith, *The History of the Chillicothe Presbytery* (Chillicothe, OH: H.W. Guthrie, Hugh Bell and Peter Platter, 1889), 8.

91. Ibid., 11.

92. Whitney R. Cross, *The Burned-Over District: The Social and Intellectual History of Enthusiastic Religion in Western New York, 1800–1850* (New York: Harper & Row, 1950), 5–6; Goodman, *Of One Blood*, 71–72; Bernard A. Weisberger, *They Gathered at the River* (Boston: Little, Brown & Company, 1958), 35, 45.

93. William Birney, *James G. Birney and His Times* (New York: D. Appleton and Company, 1890), 434.

94. Ibid.; Paul Grim, "John Rankin: Early Abolitionist," *Ohio Historical and Archaeological and Historical Quarterly* (July 1937): 238.

95. Birney, *James G. Birney and His Times*, 435.

96. William Fox Cochran, *Western Reserve and Fugitive Slave Law* (Cleveland, OH: Western Reserve Historical Society, 1920), 72.

97. Gary Knepp, *Freedom's Struggle* (Milford, OH: Little Miami Publishing Company, 2008), 94; interview with Hugh S. Fullerton, May 3, 1932, Wilbur Siebert Collection.

98. Charles G. Finney, "Letters on Revivals—No. 23," from the *Oberlin Evangelist*, January 21, 1846.

99. Weisberger, *They Gathered at the River*, 92–101.

100. Benjamin P. Thomas, *Crusader for Freedom* (New Brunswick, NJ: Rutgers University Press, 1950), 6–15.

101. Wilbur Greeley Burroughs, "Oberlin's Part in the Slavery Conflict," *Ohio Archaeological and Historical Quarterly* (July 1911): 275–76; Finney was a frequent contributor and sometime editor of *The Evangelist* and The *Oberlin Review*.

102. Samuel May, *Some Recollections of Our Anti-Slavery Conflict* (Boston: Fields, Osgood & Company, 1869), 157.

103. Dr. Isaac Beck to Wilbur Siebert, December 26, 1892, Wilbur Siebert Collection.

104. The American Colonization Society desired to send both free and enslaved blacks to Africa to form their own nation. There they would have the freedom to form a life on their own terms without the legacy of slavery hindering them. Portraying itself as an antislavery organization, its founders included Thomas Jefferson, James Madison, James Monroe,

Chief Justice John Marshall, Senator Henry Clay and Francis Scott Key. It appeared to be benevolent, but as time passed, its real motive—to purge the United States of its black people—became apparent. The society also ignored the wishes of the people it claimed to be helping. Most free blacks in the United States considered America, not Africa, their homeland.

105. Norris F. Schneider, "Zanesville Rioters Attacked Putnam Conductors of the Underground Railroad," *Zanesville News*, October 17, 1943, Wilbur Siebert Collection.

106. Thomas, *Crusader for Freedom*, 93–95.

107. *Proceedings of the Ohio Anti-Slavery Convention*, Putnam, Ohio, April 22–24, Beaumont and Wallace, printers, Wilbur Siebert Collection.

108. Schneider, "Zanesville Rioters Attacked Putnam Conductors."

109. Few realize that Weld and Birney had met two years before he attended Lane, when he was on a lecture tour commissioned by the Tappans promoting manual labor schools. Thomas, *Crusader for Freedom*, 33.

110. Henry B. Stanton, "Good News from Ohio," *The Liberator*, May 9, 1835. The *Philanthropist* became a rather notorious publication. It so enraged the community of Cincinnati that a mob broke into Birney's office and destroyed his press, tossing it in the Ohio River in 1836—repeating the event a second time one month later after he installed another one.

111. *Proceedings of the Ohio Anti-Slavery Society*, "Report of the Committee on the Condition of the People of Color in Ohio," April 22–24, 1835.

112. Birney, *James G. Birney and His Times*, 171.

113. Cross, *Burned-Over District*, 219. See Muelder, *Theodore Dwight Weld*, for detailed information on the "seventy."

114. Various sources provide estimates approximating or exceeding these numbers.

115. Henry B. Stanton, *Random Recollections* (N.p.: Macgown & Slipper, 1886), 48.

116. *Emancipator*, "Rev. Nathaniel Colver," March 2, 1837, 174.

117. *The Liberator*, January 1, 1831.

Chapter 6

118. Actually, the term was not used until 1897, according to Online Etymology Dictionary, https://www.etymonline.com/word/sodbuster.

119. Evans and Stivers, *A History of Adams County, Ohio…* (West Union, OH: E.B. Stivers, 1900), 407.

120. Ibid., 406.

121. Ibid., 409.

122. H.C. Pemberton to Wilbur Siebert, January 21, 1932, Wilbur Siebert Collection.

123. P.N. Wickerham to Wilbur Siebert, August 9, 1894, Wilbur Siebert Collection.

124. Ibid.

125. Reverend John M. McElroy to Wilbur Siebert, September 17, 1896, Wilbur Siebert Collection.

126. U.S. Census, 1840.

127. Accounts from *The Presbyterian Historical Almanac and Annual Register for 1864*, vol. 2, 1864, 136, Wilbur Siebert Collection; Reverend Samuel Crothers, DD, *Portrait and Biographical Record of the Scioto Valley, Ohio* (Chicago, 1894), 27.

128. *Presbyterian Historical Almanac...for 1864*.

129. Ibid.

130. Ann Hagedorn, *Beyond the River* (New York: Simon & Schuster, 2002), 99.

131. Interview with Joseph Stillgess by Wilbur Siebert, August 14, 1894, Wilbur Siebert Collection.

132. Dr. G.A. Harmon to Wilbur Siebert, August 20, 1894, Wilbur Siebert Collection.

133. This was an obvious reference to the American Colonization Society, which originally had been thought of as a humanitarian organization but whose motives had racist underpinnings.

134. *The Liberator*, "Chilicothe Presbytery and Slavery," May 23, 1835.

135. Tom Calarco, *The Underground Railroad and the Adirondack Region* (Jefferson, NC: McFarland and Company, 2004), 140–47; *Underground Railroad in Highland County*, DVD.

136. William Smith to Professor Willis Boughton, January 5, 1894, Wilbur Siebert Collection.

137. R.C. Rankin to Wilbur Siebert, April 8, 1892.

138. This meant being sent to work in the intensely hot cotton fields and rice paddies of the Deep South, where slaves were overworked and had a short life expectancy.

139. It was January, and Lake Erie was likely too frozen to permit travel across it.

140. McElroy to Siebert, September 17, 1896, Wilbur Siebert Collection.

141. It should be noted that this was after the passage of the infamous Fugitive Slave Act of 1850.

142. McElroy to Siebert, September 17, 1896.

143. The word used for "ruse" or "swindle" in the antebellum days.

144. Interview with Joyce Dennis, West descendant, by Tom Calarco, February 15, 2018; *Cleveland Plain Dealer*, "Digging for Full Tale of Freedom's Trail along Paint Creek," October 18, 1999; R.S. Dills, *History of Fayette County* (Dayton, OH: O'Dell & Mayer, 1881), 823.

145. Dills, *History of Fayette County*, 974.

146. *Proceedings of the Ohio Anti-Slavery Society.*

147. J.P. Stewart to Wilbur Siebert, February 16, 1896, Wilbur Siebert Collection.

148. During the 1840s, slaveholders in the counties of Carroll, Boone and Bourbon, Kentucky, learned that many of their slaves (upward of fifty) who had escaped had settled among the Quaker settlements in Cass County, Michigan. In an attempt to recover them, they planned a series of raids during which they tried to trick and surprise the residents there. The last of these three raids was in 1849. All were thwarted, but in the end, the courts awarded judgments to the slaveholders, some of whom were paid. *The History of Cass County, Michigan*, "The Underground Railroad and the Kentucky Raid" (Chicago: Waterman, Watkins & Company, 1882), 109–15.

149. *National Era*, "Proceedings of the Chillicothe Presbytery," December 4, 1851.

Chapter 7

150. Gara, *Liberty Line*, 79–81.

151. See John R. McKivigan, *The War Against Pro-Slavery Religion* (Ithaca, NY: Cornell University Press, 1974), 84–110.

152. Mrs. E.S. Shepardson to Wilbur Siebert, no date, Wilbur Siebert Collection.

153. Women in the North established numerous antislavery sewing societies just for this purpose.

154. Much of the information about the Butterworths and their involvement with the UGRR comes from two sources: Campbell's *Anti-Slavery & the Underground Railroad—Taking a Risk for Freedom: Report of the Research Committee* and Dr. Karen Dinsmore's "The Butterworth Family," Friends of the Little Miami State Park, https://littlemiamistatepark.org; interview with Dr. Karen S. Dinsmore, March 18, 2018.

155. West Virginia Tourism, "Midland Trail National Scenic Byway," https://gotowv.com/company/midland-trail-national-scenic-highway.

156. Henry T. Butterworth to Wilbur Siebert, June 9, 1892, Wilbur Siebert Collection.

157. Ibid.

158. Robert W. Carroll, "An Underground Railway: Fugitive Slaves and the Butterworths," *Cincinnati Times-Star*, August 19, 1896, Wilbur Siebert Collection.

159. Review of *The Regenerator* by William H. Burleigh, editor of the *Christian Freeman*, January 22, 1844, 14, https://popularfreethought.wordpress.com/browse-by-title/regenerator-1844-1854.

160. *Popular Free Thought* 175, "Extract from a Letter" (January 1854): 353, https://popularfreethought.wordpress.com/browse-by-title/regenerator-1844-1854.

161. Henry T. Butterworth to Wilbur Siebert, June 9, 1892, includes recollection of Jane, Wilbur Siebert Collection.

162. *(Lebanon, OH) Western Star*, "Mrs. J.F. Nicholson Gives Some Reflections," December 10, 1885; Elizabeth Nicholson to Wilbur Siebert, January 7, 1893, includes an additional memoir of Jane not part of *Western Star* article, Wilbur Siebert Collection.

163. Valentine Nicholson to Wilbur Siebert, September 10, 1892, Wilbur Siebert Collection.

164. Campbell, *Anti-Slavery & the Underground Railroad*, 251.

165. Ibid., 241.

166. Ibid., 234–39.

167. Coffin, *Reminiscences of Levi Coffin*, 549–54; Charles Theodore Greve, *Centennial History of Cincinnati and Representative Citizens* (N.p.: Biographical Pub. Company, 1904), 360–61.

168. Coffin, *Reminiscences of Levi Coffin*, 550–51.

169. Ibid., 553.

170. *(Lebanon, OH) Western Star*, "Mrs. J.F. Nicholson Gives Some Reflections."

Chapter 8

171. Smedley, *History of the Underground Railroad*, 186–87.

172. Valentine Nicholson to Wilbur Siebert, September 10, 1892, Wilbur Siebert Collection.

173. Jesse N. Oren to Clarkson Butterworth, May 23, 1892, Wilbur Siebert Collection.

174. David Monroe, a cabinetmaker in Xenia, was identified by Nicholson as being involved in the UGRR.

175. Mark Haynes to Wilbur Siebert, September 12, 1892, Wilbur Siebert Collection.

176. George M. Dakin to Wilbur Siebert, August 24, 1894, Wilbur Siebert Collection.

177. Joel P. Davis to Wilbur Siebert, August 28, 1892, Wilbur Siebert Collection.

178. J.J. Janey, a local and state government official for most of his career, said that Allen told him he had aided about 3,300 (interview with Siebert, March 24, 1892). This may be one of those apocryphal statements because Levi Coffin gave the same number whom he helped.

179. Seth Linton to Wilbur Siebert, September 4, 1892, Wilbur Siebert Collection.

180. Essie Dakin to Wilbur Siebert, October 12, 1898, Wilbur Siebert Collection; Henry T. Butterworth to Wilbur Siebert, June 9, 1892, ibid.

181. *The History of Clinton County* (Chicago: W.H. Beers and Company, 1882), 351–52.

182. Museum at the Friends Home, www.friendshomemuseum.org.

183. Campbell, *Anti-Slavery & the Underground Railroad*, 209.

184. *Selections from the Diary of Daniel Howell Hise*, "Anti-Slavery Meetings and Underground Railroad Operations" (N.p.: MacMillan Book Shop, August 5, 1933), 18–19, Wilbur Siebert Collection.

185. Frederick Douglass, *Life and Times of Frederick Douglass* (Hartford, CT: Park Publishing Company, 1881), 233.

186. According to the 1840 census, the combined population of Clinton and Warren Counties was 34,452, with 718 black.

187. Valentine Nicholson to Wilbur Siebert, September 10, 1892.

188. *Anti-Slavery Bugle*, "Slaveholders Religion," December 19, 1845.

189. A. Brooke, "Ohio and Slavery," *Anti-Slavery Bugle*, September 16, 1854; Mrs. Florence Bedford Wright, "A Station on the Underground Railroad," *Ohio Archaeological and Historical Publications* (1905): 164–69; Arnold Buffum, ed., *The Protectionist*, May 16, 1841, Wilbur Siebert Collection; *National Anti-Slavery Standard*, "Trial of A. Brooke," December 3, 1840; Essie Dakin to Wilbur Siebert, October 12, 1898; Campbell, *Anti-Slavery & the Underground Railroad*, 213–18.

190. *Huron Reflector*, "No Slavery in Ohio," May 15, 1841.

191. *Anti-Slavery Bugle*, "Ohio and Slavery," September 16, 23, 30, 1854.

192. Abram Allen and Joel P. Davis, then living in Indiana, were members of this society.
193. The *Anti-Slavery Bugle* was founded in 1845 by Abby Kelly Foster, one of William Lloyd Garrison's most trusted cohorts. It became the third of Garrison aligned abolitionist newspapers—*The Liberator*, the *National Anti-Slavery Standard* and the *Bugle*—that were the voice of the American Anti-Slavery Society.
194. D. Staley to Wilbur Siebert, September 5, 1894, Wilbur Siebert Collection.
195. All held various executive-level positions in the Western Anti-Slavery Society.
196. *Anti-Slavery Bugle*, "Salem Rescue," September 9, 1854. The *Bugle* reported another version of the story closer to the one in the Hise diary, but it was the *Herald*'s version that was reprinted in newspapers across the nation.
197. Ibid., "Popular Sentiment of Disunion," February 23, 1856.
198. Ibid., "Dr. Abram Brooke," August 14, 1858.
199. *National Anti-Slavery Standard*, "Spirit of Western Abolitionists," May 18, 1843.
200. Concord, Pennsylvania, was at about the halfway point of their journey.

Chapter 9

201. Harrold, *Subversives*; C.S. Brown, *Abel Brown Abolitionist*, annotated by Tom Calarco (Jefferson, NC: McFarland and Company, 2005).
202. There were at one time three Underground Railroad networks or Vigilance Committees in New York City, acting independently of one another, although they sometimes crossed paths. The first that formed in 1834 was the New York Committee of Vigilance with David Ruggles and Charles Ray as its leaders, until the falling out of Ruggles, who was replaced by Theodore Wright around 1840. Sidney Howard Gay's network, which began to form in the early 1840s, was more amorphous and never had a name, but it continued at least into the late 1850s. In 1846, Wright died, and in the transition, an elderly Isaac Hopper took over temporarily; the name was changed to the New York State Vigilance Committee. One year after its formation, Gerrit Smith replaced Hopper. After the Fugitive Slave Act of 1850 was passed, the Committee of Thirteen arose, composed of many of the old guard from the original Committee of Vigilance and

led by William P. Powell. The work of these committees was somewhat clandestine, although the original Committee of Vigilance issued some reports. Gay's *Record of Fugitives*, which was recently published in 2015 in *Secret Lives of the Underground Railroad in New York City* by Don Papson and Tom Calarco, provides significant insight into what the Underground Railroad did there.

203. Reverend William M. Mitchell, *The Underground Railroad* (London: William Tweedie, 1860).

204. Henry Bibb, a renowned fugitive slave himself, published a widely read and influential antislavery newspaper, the *Voice of the Fugitive*, after he escaped to Canada in 1850. It promoted the UGRR and the success of fugitives who had escaped to Canada. It ceased publication when Bibb died suddenly in 1854.

205. See R.J.M. Blackett, *Building an Antislavery Wall* (Ithaca, NY: Cornell University Press, 1983).

206. C. Peter Ripley, ed., *The Black Abolitionist Papers*, vol. 2, *Canada, 1830–1865* (Chapel Hill: University of North Carolina Press, 1986), 483.

207. W.N. Newport to Wilbur Siebert, September 16, 1895, Wilbur Siebert Collection.

208. A term commonly used to describe the capture of a fugitive from slavery.

209. *The History of Warren County, Ohio* (Chicago: W.H. Beers and Company, 1882), 586.

210. Wright, "A Station on the Underground Railroad," 167.

211. Dallas Bogan, *Warren County and Beyond* (Bowie, MD: Heritage Press, 1979), 6.

212. Jesse Wright to Wilbur Siebert, October 29, 1895, Wilbur Siebert Collection.

213. John Van Zandt of Cincinnati was convicted of aiding fugitive slaves as a result of an 1842 incident. The case broke him financially, and he died penniless five years later.

214. A. Brooke, "John McLean and Slavery," *Anti-Slavery Bugle*, April 12, 1856.

215. Joel P. Davis to Wilbur Siebert, August 28, 1892.

216. Cyrus Little to Daniel Orcutt, August 11, 1894, Wilbur Siebert Collection.

217. *(Wilmington) Herald of Freedom*, "Horrid Murder of a Colored Man," June 2, 23, 1854; November 10, 1854.

218. William Harvey to Wilbur Siebert, March 24, 1898, Wilbur Siebert Collection.

219. *Annual Report of the American Anti-Slavery Society* (New York City: William S. Dorr, 1836), 97.
220. Dr. Harvey died the following year in Kansas.
221. *(Wilmington) Herald of Freedom*, "Communications," December 12, 1851.
222. Campbell, *Anti-Slavery & the Underground Railroad*, 185–90.
223. Ibid., 150; R.G. Corwin to Wilbur Siebert, September 11, 1896, Wilbur Siebert Collection.
224. Thomas Miller to Wilbur Siebert, October 18, 1895, Wilbur Siebert Collection.
225. R.G. Corwin to Wilbur Siebert, September 11, 1896.
226. Interview with Amy Clark by Wilbur Siebert, no date, in Canada, Wilbur Siebert Collection.
227. Mrs. E.S. Shepardson to Wilbur Siebert, no date, Wilbur Siebert Collection.
228. *Anti-Slavery Bugle*, "Ohio and Slavery No II," September 23, 1854.

Chapter 10

229. Joel P. Davis and John McElroy letters to Siebert, Wilbur Siebert Collection.
230. 1850 U.S. Census.
231. Ironically, Ross and Franklin Counties, where Chilicothe and Columbus were situated, had the second- and third-highest number per capita of persons of color in the state according to the 1850 census.
232. John T. Ward to Wilbur Siebert, June 15, 1892, Wilbur Siebert Collection.
233. *The Palladium*, "Address to the Citizens of Ohio," December 27, 1843.
234. Colored Conventions: Bringing Nineteenth-Century Black Organizing to Digital Life, http://coloredconventions.org.
235. Richard Clyde Minor, "James Preston Poindexter, Elder Statesman of Columbus," *Ohio Archaeological and Historical Quarterly* (July 1947): 1–2.
236. Interview with Reverend James Poindexter by Wilbur Siebert, June 25, 1895, Wilbur Siebert Collection.
237. *History of Pickaway and Franklin Counties* (N.p.: Williams Bros., 1880), 404.
238. Cynthia Spurgeon to Wilbur Siebert, July 25, 1892, Wilbur Siebert Collection.
239. *History of Pickaway and Franklin Counties*, 406.
240. Amason Webster to Wilbur Siebert, July 25, 1892, Wilbur Siebert Collection.

241. The home of Ozem Gardner was the usual destination of fugitives sent by Bull.

242. Edward Sebring to Wilbur Siebert, no date, Wilbur Siebert Collection.

243. Interview with Ellen Reader, great-granddaughter of James Ferguson, by Wilbur Siebert, September 27, 1850.

244. See *History of Pickaway and Franklin Counties.*

245. Original Record Book, Minutes of the Anti-Slavery Society of Worthington, Ohio, March 28, 1836, Wilbur Siebert Collection.

246. Wilson Gardner to Wilbur Siebert, July 21, 1892, Wilbur Siebert Collection; Joseph Gardner to Wilbur Siebert, July 21, 1892, ibid.

247. *Sandusky Clarion*, "The Kidnappers," April 14, 1846.

248. Ibid. Craig operated the prison like a business and hired out his prisoners, like slaves, keeping their earnings for his personal income.

249. *New York Evening Post*, September 25, 1846.

250. Stephen Middleton, *Black Laws: Race and the Legal Process in Early Ohio* (Athens: University of Ohio Press, 2005), 190–95; *National Anti-Slavery Standard*, "Selections from *Philanthropist* and *Cincinnati Herald*," April 30, 1846; Leander J. Critchfield, *History of the City of Columbus*, edited by Alfred E. Lee (New York: Munsell & Company, 1892), 598–607.

251. *Ohio State Journal*, "Meeting of the Colored Men of Columbus protesting the Fugitive Slave Law," October 16, 1850.

252. The version of the account presented is based mainly on articles in the *Anti-Slavery Bugle* in April 1847 and Critchfield, *History of the City of Columbus*, 602–3.

253. This principle of law had its original precedent in the Somerset Decision of 1772, in which a slave was brought from the United States with the consent and knowledge of his owner into the free nation of England.

254. *Anti-Slavery Bugle*, "Case of Rosetta, on a Writ of Habeas Corpus," April 7, 1855.

255. Ibid.

256. See Mary Gleason McDougall, "Personal Liberty Laws," *Fugitive Slaves, 1619–1865* (Boston: Ginn & Company, 1891), 65–75.

257. *Anti-Slavery Bugle*, April 7, 1855. Historians who claim that the Underground Railroad was not a cause of the Civil War should consider this statement.

258. *Ohio Columbian*, April 8, 1855.

259. Ernest Coulter to Wilbur Siebert, May 29, 1935, Wilbur Siebert Collection.

260. The author has not been able to search this man down, but it would certainly be of interest to find him in the history books and corroborate Ernest Coulter's story.
261. For the full story of the Hanbys, see Dacia Custer Shoemaker, *Choose You This Day: The Legacy of the Hanbys*, edited by Harold B. Hancock and Millard J. Miller (Westerville, OH: Westerville Historical Society, 1983).
262. Reverend Henry Garst, DD, *Otterbein University, 1847–1907* (Dayton, OH, 1907), 138.
263. When Ben wrote the publisher asking about royalties, the publisher wrote back, "Dear Sir: Nelly Gray is sung on both sides of the Atlantic. We have made the money and you the fame—that balances the account." Fortunately, Ben wrote more songs for the publisher that were successful and for which he was financially compensated, like "Ole Shady," a song about a fugitive slave who celebrates his newfound freedom, and the Christmas classic "Up on the Rooftop."

Chapter 11

264. Cyrus Little to Wilbur Siebert, August 11, 1894, Wilbur Siebert Collection.
265. Valentine Nicholson to Wilbur Siebert, September 10, 1892; W.D. Schooley to Wilbur Siebert, November 15, 1893, Wilbur Siebert Collection.
266. *The History of Champaign County* (Chicago: W.H. Beers and Company, 1881), 604; Watts, "History of the Underground Railroad in Mechanicsburg," 211.
267. Watts, "History of the Underground Railroad in Mechanicsburg," 221–25; *History of Champaign County*, 604.
268. *History of Champaign County*, 605.
269. Ibid.; Watts, "History of the Underground Railroad in Mechanicsburg," 213.
270. Watts, "History of the Underground Railroad in Mechanicsburg," 214–18.
271. Shepherd to Siebert, July 7, 1895.
272. *Belmont Chronicle*, "Wm. M. Connelly Liberated," June 17, 1858.
273. Watts, "History of the Underground Railroad in Mechanicsburg," 218.
274. *History of Champaign County*, 605.
275. Ibid. In the Watts article, he stated that he obtained his information on William Cratty from a Newport, Kentucky resident, Mary Wanzer Furnish, who had Cratty's written records.

276. Another prolific conductor, Joseph Morris, lived about fifteen miles north of Cratty in Richland Township on the line to Sandusky.

277. *Chicago Evening Post*, "William Cratty Talks of Underground Railroad Days," July 18, 1892.

278. Griffith G. Benedict to Wilbur Siebert, December 2, 1893, Wilbur Siebert Collection.

279. Ibid.

280. Wilbur Siebert, "A Quaker Section of the Ohio Underground Railroad," *Ohio Archaeological and Historical Quarterly* (July 1930): 25.

281. Ibid., 26.

282. Aaron Benedict, "Attempting to Kidnap a Runaway Slave by Forcible Resistance, but Get the Worst of It in a Lively Melee," *Mount Gilead Sentinel*, July 27, 1893.

283. *History of Marion County* (Chicago: Leggett Conaway and Company, 1908), 363–65; Benedict, "Attempting to Kidnap a Runaway Slave."

284. M.J. Benedict to Wilbur Siebert, July 3, 1891, Wilbur Siebert Collection; Aaron Benedict, "Escape of a Slave Who Kidnaps His Family…," *Mount Gilead Sentinel*, July 27, 1893; Wilbur Siebert Collection.

285. Aaron Benedict, "One Good Deed Done by Liquor…," *Mount Gilead Sentinel*, August 13, 1893; Wilbur Siebert Collection.

286. A.L. Benedict, *Memoir of Richard Dillingham* (N.p.: Merrihew & Thompson, 1852), 3.

287. Ibid., 3–4.

288. Ibid., 10.

289. Ibid., 17.

290. His father died a few months after his sentence.

291. Benedict, *Memoir of Richard Dillingham*, 20.

292. Ibid., 6–7.

Chapter 12

293. *People's Journal*, "What the South Has Had," October 27, 1859, 2.

294. Hagedorn, *Beyond the River*, 262.

295. John Robb to Wilbur Siebert, March 11, 1896, Wilbur Siebert Collection.

296. Archy Brownlee to Wilbur Siebert, January 10, 1893, Wilbur Siebert Collection.

297. William B. Thom, "My Early Life," unpublished from the personal papers of Thom, in possession of Bertha Lillian Godfrey, Wilbur Siebert Collection.

298. Reverend George Gordon, letter to *Principia*, Iberia College newspaper, November 29, 1861.

299. A.C. Crist, ed., *History of Marion Presbytery* (N.p.: Delaware Press, 1908), 249–50.

300. William M. Cockrum, *History of the Underground Railroad: As It Was Conducted by the Anti-Slavery League* (Oakland City, IN: J.M. Cockrum Press, 1915), 9–28, 319–21.

301. Peters, "An Abolitionist," *Op. Cit:* 1,222–29.

302. According to the August 4, 1837 issue of the *The Liberator*, there were 213 antislavery societies in Ohio, with 129 accounting for their members; of those, the total was 10,162. Brown is making his statement in 1841.

303. A.B. Chambers, *Trials and Confessions of Madison Henderson, alias Blanchard, Alfred Amos Warrick, James W. Seward, and Charles Brown* (N.p.: Chambers & Knapp, 1841), 64–67.

304. This was on January 13, 1840, which is consistent with the narrative of events regarding Brown's introduction and involvement with the Ohio Anti-Slavery Society, which formed in 1835, as was seen earlier in the book.

305. Chambers, *Trials and Confessions*, 24.

306. Henry David Thoreau, *Thoreau: A Year in Thoreau's Journal, 1851* (New York: Penguin, 1993), 247.

307. Henry David Thoreau, *Civil Disobedience* (Los Angeles, CA: Enhanced Media, 2017).

308. *Cincinnati Commercial*, "A Mother's Long Search," April 9, 1892.

Appendix

309. C.B. Galbreath, "Ohio's Fugitive Slave Law," *Ohio History* 24 (1915): 226.

INDEX

ABOUT THE AUTHOR

Tom Calarco is the author/editor of seven previous books and numerous articles on the Underground Railroad. He has presented papers at the National Parks Service's "Network to Freedom" Conference and the Underground Railroad Project of the Capital Region conference and had numerous other speaking engagements. A member of the North Country Underground Railroad Historical Association, he seeks to develop the true history of the Underground Railroad.